KINGDOM PRAYERS
Prayer that works!

By Dr David Kaluba

Published by DK Global Publishing
London, United Kingdom

All scripture quotations unless otherwise mentioned are taken
from the New Kings James Version (NKJV) of the Holy Bible

ISBN-13: 9781539461500
ISBN-10: 1539461505

Contents

Introduction

I decided to write this book because after being a Christian for almost 28 years and preaching the gospel for over 25 years, I realised that it is absolutely necessary that I get this book out! For so many years, I prayed thousands of prayers out of fear, desperation, personal beliefs and sometimes even out of unbelief. Like me, there are millions of Christians out there still praying that way today. Jesus begins to give his disciples the model prayer in Matthew 6:9-12 and he begins to show how that our prayers should always be centered around the will of the Father and His kingdom. He points out that acknowledging that God is our Father was the first thing we need to do when we enter His presence. Secondly, we need to realise that our God exists outside our situation and is ultimately bigger than anything we face. He dwells in heaven and not in our situation. Heaven has a way of doing things and so the Lord points us to heaven's methodology by asking that God's will be done on earth even as it is in heaven and that His kingdom would come into every area of our lives.

I would compare this set up with an Embassy in a foreign country. While that building is in a foreign land, as soon as you go inside, you are automatically in another country and no longer live by the laws of the land where the building is physically located. In essence, while we are still in this world, we belong to another Kingdom and are only passing through. If we are to receive heavenly results as well as heavenly protection and covering, we need to find the embassy and go inside. The presence of God is our embassy, we access it through prayer and the word of God is the password! Regardless of what situation you may be going through or what challenge you face every day, the moment you enter God's presence, everything changes; your possibilities change because suddenly, all things become possible to him who believes and there is absolutely nothing too hard for our God, the King!

It is very clear that God does not respond to unbelief, fear or any of the many reasons why most of us choose to pray. He only responds to faith and faith comes by hearing His word. We can therefore, confidently say that God only listens to faith prayers, which are essentially prayers made in line with His will, which is in His word; I call these, Kingdom Prayers! The written word of God is the Logos, which is the Greek word for the written word of God. However, as soon as you open your mouth and begin to speak it out loud, the same word is transformed into the Rhema word of God, which is the Greek word for the spoken word of God. The power behind the word is activated with your voice. What about those who cannot speak you ask? God can still hear even without being loud in the same way He heard Hannah when she prayed for a son in 1 Samuel 1:13, the Bible says she prayed with her heart and her lips were moving though no words came out. The woman with the issue of blood also said in her heart that she would be healed if only she could touch the helm of the Lord's garment. So you can therefore, pray with your heart but whatever you do, say something! This is why the Bible says that the word of God is a more sure word of prophecy, even better than the word of prophecy you might receive from an earthly prophet and it is available to everyone who believes both small and great. The time has come for you to search out the scriptures that pattern to your specific situation and see a flood of breakthrough come your way. I hear the sound of an abundance of rain because it is about to pour showers of blessing your way.

In Matthew 6:9-13, we see the model of prayer outlined showing us how we ought to pray and not necessarily in those exact words. This model is the fulfilment of the Tabernacle as given to Moses under the old covenant: "In this manner, therefore, pray: Our Father in heaven, Hallowed be Your name. Your kingdom come. Your will be done on earth as it is in heaven. Give us this day our daily bread. And forgive us our debts, as we forgive our debtors. And do not lead us into temptation, but deliver us from the evil one. For Yours is the kingdom and the power and the glory forever. Amen." - Matthew 6:5-13 NKJV

We find the description of the Lord's Prayer portrayed in the type and shadow that is the Tabernacle in Exodus 26:31-35: ""You shall make a veil woven of blue, purple, and scarlet thread, and fine woven linen. It shall be woven with an artistic design of cherubim. You shall hang it upon the four pillars of acacia wood overlaid with gold. Their hooks shall be gold, upon four sockets of silver. And you shall hang the veil from the clasps. Then you shall bring the ark of the Testimony in there, behind the veil. The veil shall be a divider for you between the holy place and the Most Holy. You shall put the mercy seat upon the ark of the Testimony in the Most Holy. You shall set the table outside the veil, and the lamp-stand across from the table on the side of the tabernacle toward the south; and you shall put the table on the north side." - Exodus 26:31-35 NKJV

We are to always come before the LORD with thanksgiving followed by praise before making any requests or even asking for forgiveness. Enter His gates with thanksgiving in your heart and then begin to praise your way into the holy place. As you progress into worship, the door into the holy of hollies opens up and it is here that we find God's Shekinah glory, which is the palatable version of the glory of God, for human beings are not wired to meet with God face to face and live to testify about it.

Preface

I have heard so many prayers from saints all over the world and many of our Christian family pray mostly out of necessity or need. This book is designed to change that by showing how to pray the perfect will of God using His perfect word. The greatest motivation is to see as many people empowered as possible, it is the will of God that we win in this life and what better way to win than to live a life of answered prayer! I would have loved to include as many scriptures as possible however, it is impossible to completely cover every issue that life throws at us without writing the biggest book in the world. My prayer for you is that after reading this book, your eyes of understanding will be opened to this amazing realm that is a life of answered prayer. You may use this book as a personal or family daily devotion or just as a friend in need whenever you need to pray about almost anything. If for some reason, you do not find the specific prayer point you need to pray about, simply use the same pattern and go through the scriptures to find a word that talks about your situation. There is absolutely nothing in life that you can ever go through that is not documented in the Bible, for it is given for correction and edification. I am forever grateful for the love and support that I have received while taking time out to write this precious book from my family and friends without whom this book would certainly not be possible! Thank you from the bottom of my heart, may God continue to increase you more and more.

Synopsis

Are you ready to really touch heaven and experience a life full of blessing and answered prayer; ready to take your prayer life to the next level and speak God's language? Then you could not be holding a better book in your hands right now; Kingdom Prayers is a book that will change your life forever by showing you step by step, how to apply a specific word to specific real life issues of everyday life! Jesus said that people do not get their prayers answered firstly because they do not ask and that is why he says ask and it shall be given, knock and the door shall be opened, seek and you shall certainly find. But the second and just as important reason is that people pray amiss. By praying amiss, the Lord was referring to prayers made outside the premise and blessing of the word of God, which houses the will of God and ties Him to His own covenant. It is impossible for God to break His own covenant, which He ratified in His own blood swearing upon Himself as He could not find anyone greater to swear by. The only way God will negate His word is by denying Himself. This is exciting because it means that as long as you pray the perfect will of God embedded in His word, His promises to you are forever yea and Amen! And this is the confidence that we have, that when we ask, He hears us. Thank God we have a savior, whose ear is not too deaf to hear nor His hand too short to save. As if that were not good enough, the Bible tells us that He is not a man that He should lie, since He said it, He will bring it to pass and since He promised it, He will sure follow through and make it happen for you. Welcome to a life of answered prayer!

The Issues of life:

As you continue working through this book, you will find that most of the scriptures are direct prayers in themselves and there is no need to chance them at all. However, do feel free to personalise each prayer point using the scripture(s) given to pray in line with the word. Here is an example of how to use the scriptures wherever the prayer point does not seem to be straight forward:

Anxiety

Romans 8.28
"And we know that all things work together for good to those who love God, to those who are the called according to His purpose." - Romans 8:28 NKJV

Prayer

Lord, I know that things seem really hard for me right now and sometimes I cannot even make sense of my situation but I thank you that your word says all things are working together for my good right now. I love you Lord and I receive my breakthrough in Jesus' name!

Enjoy the rest of this precious book even as the Holy Spirit helps you with understanding and stay blessed always:

Abuse

Psalm 23:5
"You prepare a table before me in the presence of my enemies; You anoint my head with oil; my cup runs over." - Psalms 23:5 NKJV

Psalm 103:6
"The LORD executes righteousness and justice for all who are oppressed." - Psalms 103:6 NKJV

Prayer

Thank you LORD for your grace and for having my back regardless of what is happening around me. You will not leave me defenseless but will fight for me and deal with my oppressors, for you are the God who dispenses justice for all the oppressed and I believe that you are preparing a table for me right now even as my enemies look on. I receive your grace, favour and protection in Jesus' name!

Accommodation

Acts 17:26
"And He has made from one blood every nation of men to dwell on all the face of the earth, and has determined their pre-appointed times and the boundaries of their dwellings," - Acts 17:26 NKJV

Prayer

LORD, I know that you know everything about me. You pre-determined my exact address and physical location at any one point in my life, I thank you that I will never be homeless because you will make a way for me even where there seems to be no way. By faith, I call forth and receive my home right now in Jesus' name.

Addiction

1 Corinthians 10:13
"No temptation has overtaken you except such as is common to man; but God is faithful, who will not allow you to be tempted beyond what you are able, but with the temptation will also make the way of escape, that you may be able to bear it." - I Corinthians 10:13 NKJV

Prayer

Dear Daddy, this is a hard one for me as I am struggling with letting go of this bad habit and I desperately need your help! I know that with every temptation I face, you will always provide a way out for me. Please give me the strength and the courage to say no and to stand my ground. Thank you LORD that when I am weak then I am really strong because your strength is made perfect in my weakness. I receive your love and help in my situation and I thank you that my last word shall be victory!

Ageing

Proverbs 16:31
"The silver-haired head is a crown of glory, if it is found in the way of righteousness." - Proverbs 16:31 NKJV

Psalm 92:14-15
"They shall still bear fruit in old age; they shall be fresh and flourishing, to declare that the LORD is upright; He is my rock, and there is no unrighteousness in Him." - Psalms 92:14-15 NKJV

Prayer

Thank you LORD, for you will crown my head with glory, and I will still be fruitful in my old age. I will live long and strong and will flourish in the earth to show that you are a good Father. People will look at me and declare that I am the blessed of the LORD. You are my rock and you always do the right thing, I trust you and receive your kindness even as you enable me to fulfill my purpose in the earth.

Angels

Psalm 91:11-12
"For He shall give His angels charge over you, to keep you in all your ways. In their hands they shall bear you up, lest you dash your foot against a stone." - Psalms 91:11-12 NKJV

Prayer

Many things happen around me all the time and right now I feel like I am in between a hard place and a rock but I rejoice in the knowledge that you are always with me and you have even sent angels to watch over me. Your angels go before me to clear any traps that have been set for me and none of them will trip me up! Thank you LORD.

Anger

Proverbs 14:29
"He who is slow to wrath has great understanding, but he who is impulsive exalts folly." - Proverbs 14:29 NKJV

James 1:20
"for the wrath of man does not produce the righteousness of God." - James 1:20 NKJV

Prayer

There are some people that just get to me all the time LORD and sometimes I find it really hard to just ignore their offenses and I lose it like right now! But I know that my wrath does not please you nor produce your righteousness, please help me to be slow to anger and control my temper; that I may not be impulsive in my actions but that I may with patience deal with all my challenges. I receive self-control and peace in Jesus' name.

Answers

2 Corinthians1:20
"For all the promises of God in Him are Yes, and in Him Amen, to the glory of God through us." - II Corinthians 1:20 NKJV

Psalm 91:15
"He shall call upon Me, and I will answer him; I will be with him in trouble; I will deliver him and honour him." - Psalms 91:15 NKJV

Isaiah 65:24

""It shall come to pass that before they call, I will answer; And while they are still speaking, I will hear." Isaiah 65:24 NKJV

Jeremiah 33:2-3

""Thus says the LORD who made it, the LORD who formed it to establish it (the LORD is His name): 'Call to Me, and I will answer you, and show you great and mighty things, which you do not know.'" - Jeremiah 33:2-3 NKJV

Prayer

Your word Oh LORD says that when I call, you will answer me, that you already know my prayer even before I open my mouth. I thank you that you always hear me and your answers to me are always yes and amen! Answer me in my trouble Oh LORD, for I am in trouble and I need you more than ever! You are the God who knows all things and opens doors that no man can shut, I receive answers now in Jesus' name and I know what to do when I don't know what to do.

Anxiety

Romans 8.28

"And we know that all things work together for good to those who love God, to those who are the called according to His purpose." - Romans 8:28 NKJV

Matthew 6:31-34

""Therefore do not worry, saying, 'What shall we eat?' or 'What shall we drink?' or 'What shall we wear?' For after all these things the Gentiles seek. For your heavenly Father knows that you need all these things. But seek first the kingdom of God and His righteousness, and all these things shall be added to you. Therefore do not worry about tomorrow, for tomorrow will worry about its own things. Sufficient for the day is its own trouble." - Matthew 6:31-34 NKJV

Philippians 4:6-7
"Be anxious for nothing, but in everything by prayer and supplication, with thanksgiving, let your requests be made known to God; and the peace of God, which surpasses all understanding, will guard your hearts and minds through Christ Jesus." - Philippians 4:6-7 NKJV

Prayer

Things have been tough lately and sometimes, I don't even know whether I am coming or going! But I thank you that you cause all things to work together for my good because I love you. I refuse to worry about anything as I trust you with my life and I know that you can never mismanage it! Although I am troubled by many things right now, I refuse to panic because I know that you know that I need all these things, so today, I choose to seek your face instead. You've got my back and I thank you.

Babies

Psalm 127:3-5
"Behold, children are a heritage from the LORD, The fruit of the womb is a reward. Like arrows in the hand of a warrior, so are the children of one's youth. Happy is the man who has his quiver full of them; They shall not be ashamed, But shall speak with their enemies in the gate." - Psalms 127:3-5 NKJV

Prayer

LORD, please watch over my children as I cannot always be there to see everything. Help me to guide them in the way that they should go and give me the wisdom and grace that I need to direct them in the way more perfect. I believe I receive favour for my children and my children's children.

Barrenness

Deuteronomy 7:14
"You shall be blessed above all peoples; there shall not be a male or female barren among you or among your livestock." - Deuteronomy 7:14 NKJV

Galatians 4:27
"For it is written: "Rejoice, O barren, you who do not bear! Break forth and shout, you who are not in labour! For the desolate has many more children than she who has a husband."" - Galatians 4:27 NKJV

Prayer

I receive the fruit of the womb and declare that barrenness is not my portion! I rejoice in advance for my harvest and thank you for your faithfulness and kindness towards me.

Bereavement

Psalm 116:8
"For You have delivered my soul from death, my eyes from tears, and my feet from falling." - Psalms 116:8 NKJV

2 Corinthians 1:3-5

"Blessed be the God and Father of our Lord Jesus Christ, the Father of mercies and God of all comfort, who comforts us in all our tribulation, that we may be able to comfort those who are in any trouble, with the comfort with which we ourselves are comforted by God. For as the sufferings of Christ abound in us, so our consolation also abounds through Christ." - II Corinthians 1:3-5 NKJV

1 Thessalonians 4:13-18

"But I do not want you to be ignorant, brethren, concerning those who have fallen asleep, lest you sorrow as others who have no hope. For if we believe that Jesus died and rose again, even so God will bring with Him those who sleep in Jesus. For this we say to you by the word of the Lord, that we who are alive and remain until the coming of the Lord will by no means precede those who are asleep. For the Lord Himself will descend from heaven with a shout, with the voice of an archangel, and with the trumpet of God. And the dead in Christ will rise first. Then we who are alive and remain shall be caught up together with them in the clouds to meet the Lord in the air. And thus we shall always be with the Lord. Therefore comfort one another with these words." - I Thessalonians 4:13-18 NKJV

Prayer

Thank you that you comfort me when I need you the most and if ever there was a time that I needed you the most, this is it LORD. I am sad because I have lost a loved one and am struggling to retain my joy even though I know that your joy is my strength. Strengthen me Oh LORD and give me courage to carry on; help me celebrate life instead knowing fully well that I will see my loved one again when you return in glory. Though my eyes are full of tears today, I know that you are with me and your love will see me through. Thank you LORD for being the best Father ever!

Bitterness

Proverbs 28:13
"He who covers his sins will not prosper, but whoever confesses and forsakes them will have mercy." - Proverbs 28:13 NKJV

Psalm 51:10
"Create in me a clean heart, O God, and renew a steadfast spirit within me." - Psalms 51:10 NKJV

Colossians 3:12-17
"Therefore, as the elect of God, holy and beloved, put on tender mercies, kindness, humility, meekness, long-suffering; bearing with one another, and forgiving one another, if anyone has a complaint against another; even as Christ forgave you, so you also must do. But above all these things put on love, which is the bond of perfection. And let the peace of God rule in your hearts, to which also you were called in one body; and be thankful. Let the word of Christ dwell in you richly in all wisdom, teaching and admonishing one another in psalms and hymns and spiritual songs, singing with grace in your hearts to the Lord. And whatever you do in word or deed, do all in the name of the Lord Jesus, giving thanks to God the Father through Him." - Colossians 3:12-17 NKJV

Prayer

LORD, help me to let this go! Help me to forgive please, that I may not remain bitter especially as I believe that I was right! I pray that your peace alone will reign in my heart and that your word will dwell in me so richly and deeply that I will have no room for bitterness. Thank you for the strength and courage to let it go in Jesus' name!

Blessing

Galatians 3:13-14
"Christ has redeemed us from the curse of the law, having become a curse for us (for it is written, "Cursed is everyone who hangs on a tree"), that the blessing of Abraham might come upon the Gentiles in Christ Jesus, that we might receive the promise of the Spirit through faith." - Galatians 3:13-14 NKJV

Numbers 6:24-26
""The LORD bless you and keep you; The LORD make His face shine upon you, and be gracious to you; The LORD lift up His countenance upon you, And give you peace." "" - Numbers 6:24-26 NKJV

Deuteronomy 28:1-13
""Now it shall come to pass, if you diligently obey the voice of the LORD your God, to observe carefully all His commandments which I command you today, that the LORD your God will set you high above all nations of the earth. And all these blessings shall come upon you and overtake you, because you obey the voice of the LORD your God: "Blessed shall you be in the city, and blessed shall you be in the country. "Blessed shall be the fruit of

your body, the produce of your ground and the increase of your herds, the increase of your cattle and the offspring of your flocks. "Blessed shall be your basket and your kneading bowl. "Blessed shall you be when you come in, and blessed shall you be when you go out. "The LORD will cause your enemies who rise against you to be defeated before your face; they shall come out against you one way and flee before you seven ways. "The LORD will command the blessing on you in your storehouses and in all to which you set your hand, and He will bless you in the land which the LORD your God is giving you. "The LORD will establish you as a holy people to Himself, just as He has sworn to you, if you keep the commandments of the LORD your God and walk in His ways. Then all peoples of the earth shall see that you are called by the name of the LORD, and they shall be afraid of you. And the LORD will grant you plenty of goods, in the fruit of your body, in the increase of your livestock, and in the produce of your ground, in the land of which the LORD swore to your fathers to give you. The LORD will open to you His good treasure, the heavens, to give the rain to your land in its season, and to bless all the work of your hand. You shall lend to many nations, but you shall not borrow. And the LORD will make you the head and not the tail; you shall be above only, and not be beneath, if you heed the commandments of the LORD your God, which I command you today, and are careful to observe them." - Deuteronomy 28:1-13 NKJV

Prayer

Thank you LORD that I have been redeemed from the curse of the law because I am saved! When you bless a man or woman, nobody can curse the blessed of the LORD and that means there is only goodness in my future. Thank you that you will bless me and keep me; that you will cause your face to shine upon me and be gracious to me; you give me peace and bless all the work of my hands. I am blessed everywhere I go, whether I am in the city or the country, whether I come in or go out; your blessings follow me and surround me on my left, my right, behind me and in front of me. Thank you LORD for your blessing, which makes me rich and adds no sorrow with it!

Bullying

Psalm 91:1-7
"He who dwells in the secret place of the Most High Shall abide under the shadow of the Almighty. I will say of the LORD, "He is my refuge and my fortress; My God, in Him I will trust." Surely He shall deliver you from the snare of the fowler and from the perilous pestilence. He shall cover you with His feathers, and under His wings you shall take refuge; His truth shall be your shield and buckler. You shall not be afraid of the terror by night, nor of the arrow that flies by day, Nor of the pestilence that walks in darkness, Nor of the destruction that lays waste at noonday. A thousand may fall at your side, and ten thousand at your right hand; But it shall not come near you." - Psalms 91:1-7 NKJV

Psalm 27:1-3
"The LORD is my light and my salvation; Whom shall I fear? The LORD is the strength of my life; Of whom shall I be afraid? When the wicked came against me to eat up my flesh, my enemies and foes, they stumbled and fell. Though an army may encamp against me, my heart shall not fear;

Though war may rise against me, in this I will be confident." - Psalms 27:1-3 NKJV

Prayer

I refuse to fear regardless of what enemies surround me because I dwell in the secret place of the Most High! It does not matter whether it is day time or dark in the night, I will not fear for Oh LORD are my shield, my light and my salvation. The wicked will come and try to unsettle me and bully me around but you will cause them to stumble and fall, my confidence is in you and you alone. A thousand may fall on my side and ten thousand on my side, but no harm will come near me. Thank you that my last word shall be victory, for you have put a hedge of protection around me and that my soul knows very well!

Business

Deuteronomy 28:8
""The LORD will command the blessing on you in your storehouses and in all to which you set your hand, and He will bless you in the land which the LORD your God is giving you." - Deuteronomy 28:8 NKJV

Proverbs 22:29
"Do you see a man who excels in his work? He will stand before kings; He will not stand before unknown men." - Proverbs 22:29 NKJV

Isaiah 48:17
"Thus says the LORD, your Redeemer, The Holy One of Israel: "I am the LORD your God, Who teaches you to

profit, Who leads you by the way you should go." - Isaiah 48:17 NKJV

Prayer

I have the anointing of the entrepreneur because you Oh LORD teach me to profit and prosper, I will excel in my work and stand before royalty because you have commanded the blessing on me and have blessed my savings and investments; everything I touch will prosper because you bless the work of my hand and everything I touch will turn to gold!Give me wisdom and favour to prosper that I may be your distribution centre in the earth. I believe that I receive business success now in Jesus' name.

Career

Ecclesiastes 11:6
"In the morning sow your seed, and in the evening do not withhold your hand; for you do not know which will prosper, either this or that, or whether both alike will be good." - Ecclesiastes 11:6 NKJV

Job 22:28-29
"You will also declare a thing, and it will be established for you; so light will shine on your ways. When they cast you down, and you say, 'Exaltation will come! ' Then He will save the humble person." - Job 22:28-29 NKJV

Proverbs 16:3
"Commit your works to the LORD, and your thoughts will be established." - Proverbs 16:3 NKJV

Prayer

Lord, I commit my career into your hands for your word says that when I do so, my work will be established! I also decree and declare today that I am fruitful and successful even as I continue to sow good seeds of hard work and diligence into my career. Thank you that exaltation will come to me and your will promote me with more honour. I believe I receive the end of my faith in Jesus' name!

Children

Psalm 127:3-5
"Behold, children are a heritage from the LORD, The fruit of the womb is a reward. Like arrows in the hand of a warrior, so are the children of one's youth. Happy is the man who has his quiver full of them; they shall not be ashamed, But shall speak with their enemies in the gate." - Psalms 127:3-5 NKJV

Psalm 112:2
"His descendants will be mighty on earth; the generation of the upright will be blessed." - Psalms 112:2 NKJV

Isaiah 54:13-14
"All your children shall be taught by the LORD, and great shall be the peace of your children. In righteousness you shall be established; you shall be far from oppression, for you shall not fear; and from terror, for it shall not come near you." - Isaiah 54:13-14 NKJV

Prayer

Thank you LORD that my children shall be mighty in the earth and great shall be their peace. No oppression will come anywhere near them and they shall never walk in fear for no harm will come near them. Thank you Lord for protecting my inheritance and legacy.

Clothes

Matthew 6:28-32
""So why do you worry about clothing? Consider the lilies of the field, how they grow: they neither toil nor spin; and yet I say to you that even Solomon in all his glory was not arrayed like one of these. Now if God so clothes the grass of the field, which today is, and tomorrow is thrown into the oven, will He not much more clothe you, O you of little faith? "Therefore do not worry, saying, 'What shall we eat?' or 'What shall we drink?' or 'What shall we wear?' For after all these things the Gentiles seek. For your heavenly Father knows that you need all these things." - Matthew 6:28-32 NKJV

Prayer

Lord I believe that I will never be without clothing for you take care of even my wardrobe. There is nothing about my life that you do not care about so I refuse to worry about what I shall wear for you alone are my provider. You even help me pick the right clothes for me; clothes that compliment me and my shape to reveal all my glory.

Confusion

1 Corinthians 14:33
"For God is not the author of confusion but of peace, as in all the churches of the saints." - I Corinthians 14:33 NKJV

Prayer

Lord, you are not the God of confusion; therefore, I thank you that I have peace, with nothing missing and nothing broken. I have peace of mind and know what to do when I don't know what to do. I receive all wisdom and clarity in my situation now in Jesus' name!

Contentment

Hebrews 13:5-6
"Let your conduct be without covetousness; be content with such things as you have. For He Himself has said, "I will never leave you nor forsake you." So we may boldly say: "The LORD is my helper; I will not fear. What can man do to me?"" - Hebrews 13:5-6 NKJV

Philippians 4:11
"Not that I speak in regard to need, for I have learned in whatever state I am, to be content:"-Philippians 4:11 NKJV

Ecclesiastes 3:12
"I know that nothing is better for them than to rejoice, and to do good in their lives," - Ecclesiastes 3:12 NKJV

Prayer

Daddy LORD, I know that I do not have everything I want and sometimes I really wish I could but I know that it is okay not to have everything all at once. Teach me to be content with my life and to be grateful with all that you have given me. I know that you've got my back and will never mismanage my life, thank you LORD.

Courage

Joshua 1:9
"Have I not commanded you? Be strong and of good courage; do not be afraid, nor be dismayed, for the LORD your God is with you wherever you go."" - Joshua 1:9 NKJV

Psalm 27:14
"Wait on the LORD; be of good courage, and He shall strengthen your heart; Wait, I say, on the LORD!" - Psalms 27:14 NKJV

Psalm 31:24
"Be of good courage, And He shall strengthen your heart, all you who hope in the LORD." - Psalms 31:24 NKJV

Prayer

I thank you LORD that I have the courage that I need to face all of life, for you have equipped me with power and authority to win. I am not afraid but am strong and courageous in you for you are my pillar of strength and my rock! And there is no fear in love; You Oh LORD are love.

Covenant

Ezekiel 16:60
""Nevertheless I will remember My covenant with you in the days of your youth, and I will establish an everlasting covenant with you." - Ezekiel 16:60 NKJV

Prayer

Faithful God, The one who keeps covenant to a thousand generations, thank you that You remain faithful to me despite myself and Your blessing over my life is everlasting. I am at rest because I know that you are always with me come rain come sunshine.

Danger

Psalm 34:7-8
"The angel of the LORD encamps all around those who fear Him, and delivers them. Oh, taste and see that the LORD is good; Blessed is the man who trusts in Him!" - Psalms 34:7-8 NKJV

Psalm 91:1-2
"He who dwells in the secret place of the Most High Shall abide under the shadow of the Almighty. I will say of the LORD, "He is my refuge and my fortress; My God, in Him I will trust."" - Psalms 91:1-2 NKJV

Psalm 23:4-5
"Yea, though I walk through the valley of the shadow of death, I will fear no evil; For You are with me; Your rod and Your staff, they comfort me. You prepare a table before

me in the presence of my enemies; You anoint my head with oil; My cup runs over." - Psalms 23:4-5 NKJV

Psalm 32:7
"You are my hiding place; You shall preserve me from trouble; You shall surround me with songs of deliverance. Selah" - Psalms 32:7 NKJV

Prayer

Oh LORD, you are my hiding place and in times of danger and trouble, I find refuge in you. It does not matter what is happening around me or who is planning evil against me, they shall not come anywhere near me for you are my refuge and my fortress! Even though I walk through scary situations and I get tired, I refuse to fear because your protection is out of this world. You keep me from trouble and I rejoice in advance because I trust you completely.

Dating

1 Corinthians 15:33
"Do not be deceived: "Evil company corrupts good habits."" - I Corinthians 15:33 NKJV

Philippians 2:4
"Let each of you look out not only for his own interests, but also for the interests of others."
Philippians 2:4 NKJV

Prayer

LORD, as I look forward to my life's companion, I thank you that you have prepared the right person just for me and you will move heaven and earth to ensure that my companion is in the right place and at the right time just for me; all beautiful and to my specifications for you grant me the desires of my heart. I thank you that I am a good judge of character and will know when a time-waster comes my way. Give me the wisdom to discern when my blessings come my way that I may respond accordingly Oh LORD.

Death

Psalm 116:15
"Precious in the sight of the LORD Is the death of His saints." - Psalms 116:15 NKJV

Philippians 1:21
For to me, to live *is* Christ, and to die *is* gain. – Philippians 1:21 NKJV

1 Corinthians 15:55-57
""O Death, where is your sting? O Hades, where is your victory?" The sting of death is sin, and the strength of sin is the law. But thanks be to God, who gives us the victory through our Lord Jesus Christ." - I Corinthians 15:55-57 NKJV

Prayer

Before I come home to be with you Lord, please let me fulfil my purpose in the earth. For, for me to live is Christ and to die is gain! I know that my departure from the earth is sweet in your sight but I refuse to die before my time and no sickness or devil in hell shall take me out before my time! I will live and not die before my time and will surely see your goodness in the land of the living. I believe it and I receive in Jesus' name!

Debt

Proverbs 22:7
"The rich rules over the poor, And the borrower is servant to the lender." - Proverbs 22:7 NKJV

Prayer

Daddy, you are the richest being ever and I am your child, your word tells me that I am the head and not the tail and since the rich rule over the poor, I am convinced that I am not meant to be broke and this is only a temporary situation. Since I have whatever I say, I decree and declare that I am debt-free; thatI am a lender and not a borrower; that all my needs are met and I have overflow to be a blessing to other in Jesus' name!

Deliverance

Psalm 3:8
"Salvation belongs to the LORD. Your blessing is upon Your people. Selah" - Psalms 3:8 NKJV

Psalm 18:2-3
"The LORD is my rock and my fortress and my deliverer; My God, my strength, in whom I will trust; My shield and the horn of my salvation, my stronghold. I will call upon the LORD, who is worthy to be praised; So shall I be saved from my enemies." - Psalms 18:2-3 NKJV

Prayer

Save me Oh LORD and I will be saved, set me free and I will be free! You are my rock and my fortress, I trust you with my life and I call upon you today for you are worthy. Save me from my enemies that your name may be glorified in all the earth. Do not put me to shame Oh LORD and deliver me from my adversaries and issues that hold me down. I believe I receive in Jesus' name!

Depression

John 16:33
"These things I have spoken to you, that in Me you may have peace. In the world you will have tribulation; but be of good cheer, I have overcome the world."" - John 16:33 NKJV

2 Corinthians 7:6
"Nevertheless God, who comforts the downcast, comforted us by the coming of Titus," - II Corinthians 7:6 NKJV

Psalm 43:5
"Why are you cast down, O my soul? And why are you disquieted within me? Hope in God; For I shall yet praise Him, The help of my countenance and my God." - Psalms 43:5 NKJV

Nehemiah 8:10
"Then he said to them, "Go your way, eat the fat, drink the sweet, and send portions to those for whom nothing is prepared; for this day is holy to our Lord. Do not sorrow, for the joy of the LORD is your strength."" - Nehemiah 8:10 NKJV

Prayer

Thank you LORD that in you I have peace regardless of what is happening around me. I thank you that sorrow is not my portion, your joy is my strength and you comfort me in times of trouble. I refuse to be cast down in my soul and feel sorry for myself for I am the redeemed of the LORD and I say so! I receive supernatural joy now in Jesus' name.

Direction

Proverbs 3:5
"Trust in the LORD with all your heart, and lean not on your own understanding;" - Proverbs 3:5 NKJV

Isaiah 30:21
"Your ears shall hear a word behind you, saying, "This is the way, walk in it," Whenever you turn to the right hand or whenever you turn to the left." - Isaiah 30:21 NKJV

Prayer

I have some very important decisions to make right now Daddy and to be quite honest; I do not really know what I need to do or what I can do. Your word says that you will show me the way I should go and today I need direction Lord, Show me what I need to do, give me the words I should speak and help me make the right decision for you Oh LORD know all things and you can never mismanage my life. I receive answers now in Jesus' name.

Discontentment

Psalm 43:5
"Why are you cast down, O my soul? And why are you disquieted within me? Hope in God; For I shall yet praise Him, The help of my countenance and my God." - Psalms 43:5 NKJV

Prayer

Teach me to be content in all things Lord and to count my blessings instead of my problems; teach me to focus on the size of my God and not the size of my issues; to listen to your voice and your word more than I listen to my accusers.

Discouragement

Psalm 42:11
"Why are you cast down, O my soul? And why are you disquieted within me? Hope in God; For I shall yet praise Him, The help of my countenance and my God." - Psalms 42:11 NKJV

Ephesians 3:13
"Therefore I ask that you do not lose heart at my tribulations for you, which is your glory." - Ephesians 3:13 NKJV

Prayer

I feel so discouraged right now and it just seems like things just keep getting worse. Lord, you are the help of my countenance and I refuse to lose heart. Strengthen me and I will be strong, for you are my rock and my salvation.

Disappointment

Psalm 20:7
"Some trust in chariots, and some in horses; But we will remember the name of the LORD our God. They have bowed down and fallen; But we have risen and stand upright. Save, LORD! May the King answer us when we call." - Psalms 20:7-9 NKJV

Prayer

Some trust in all sorts of things and I admit that I myself have trusted in my own strength sometimes and have found myself let down. But today, I choose to put my trust only in you Oh LORD. And I refuse to give up for You did not bring me this far just to leave me stranded. I can never and will never be stuck. Thank you Lord.

Doubt

Mark 11:24
"Therefore I say to you, whatever things you ask when you pray, believe that you receive them, and you will have them." - Mark 11:24 NKJV

Isaiah 41:10
"Fear not, for I am with you; Be not dismayed, for I am your God. I will strengthen you, Yes, I will help you, I will uphold you with My righteous right hand.'" - Isaiah 41:10 NKJV

Prayer

I know that doubt is not my friend LORD but sometimes I am just not sure like right now. My faith is weak and I need you LORD, please help my unbelief. Strengthen me and uphold me with your righteous hand that I may not lose it. Help me see past all the evidence and put my trust completely in you. Thank you for giving me the gift of faith and for being my rock in my time of weakness.

Encouragement

Proverbs 3:5-6
"Trust in the LORD with all your heart, and lean not on your own understanding; In all your ways acknowledge Him, And He shall direct your paths." - Proverbs 3:5-6 NKJV

Proverbs 18:10
"The name of the LORD is a strong tower; The righteous run to it and are safe." - Proverbs 18:10 NKJV

Psalm 55:22
"Cast your burden on the LORD, And He shall sustain you; He shall never permit the righteous to be moved." - Psalms 55:22 NKJV

Isaiah 41:10
"Fear not, for I am with you; Be not dismayed, for I am your God. I will strengthen you, Yes, I will help you, I will uphold you with My righteous right hand.'" - Isaiah 41:10 NKJV

Prayer

I surrender to you and cast my burdens on you LORD. You are my God and will not allow me to be moved, You will strengthen and help me; You will never let me fall completely to the ground nor allow me to sink in my trouble, Your right hand will always pull me up absolutely!

Enemies

Psalm 23:5
"You prepare a table before me in the presence of my enemies; You anoint my head with oil; My cup runs over."
- Psalms 23:5 NKJV

Psalm 27:1-3
"The LORD is my light and my salvation; Whom shall I fear? The LORD is the strength of my life; Of whom shall I be afraid? When the wicked came against me to eat up my flesh, my enemies and foes, they stumbled and fell. Though an army may encamp against me, my heart shall not fear; Though war may rise against me, in this I will be confident." - Psalms 27:1-3 NKJV

Prayer

I wish I had no enemies Lord but I thank you that they will not win over me, for you are preparing a table for me right now in their very presence. They will look at me and exclaim that I am the blessed of the LORD! You are my light and my salvation and I am not afraid. Though the wicked may come up against me to destroy me, they will stumble and fall. Thank you that I am safe in you oh LORD and my last word shall be victory.

Envy

Proverbs 23:17
"Do not let your heart envy sinners, But be zealous for the fear of the LORD all the day;" - Proverbs 23:17 NKJV

1 Corinthians 13:4
"Love suffers long and is kind; love does not envy; love does not parade itself, is not puffed up;" - I Corinthians 13:4 NKJV

Prayer

Sometimes I want what other people have Lord, but I know that you have a path mapped out specifically for me so please help me to be content with my lot. Help me celebrate the success of others and pray for them instead of walking in envy, may Your love fill my heart that I may walk in humility and not be puffed up in Jesus' name.

Exams

1 Thessalonians 3:5
"For this reason, when I could no longer endure it, I sent to know your faith, lest by some means the tempter had tempted you, and our labor might be in vain." - I Thessalonians 3:5 NKJV

2 Corinthians 12:9
"And He said to me, "My grace is sufficient for you, for My strength is made perfect in weakness." Therefore most gladly I will rather boast in my infirmities, that the power of Christ may rest upon me." - II Corinthians 12:9 NKJV

Prayer

Sometimes I get so tired of revising and find it hard to endure but thank you that your grace is sufficient for me. Your strength is made perfect in my weakness and therefore, I believe that I will be successful in my exams. Thank you that my memory and understanding are sharpened and I have the intelligence I need to excel.

Failure

2 Corinthians 4:16-17
"Therefore we do not lose heart. Even though our outward man is perishing, yet the inward man is being renewed day by day. For our light affliction, which is but for a moment, is working for us a far more exceeding and eternal weight of glory," - II Corinthians 4:16-17 NKJV

Psalm 73:26
"But it is good for me to draw near to God; I have put my trust in the Lord GOD, that I may declare all Your works." - Psalms 73:28 NKJV

Prayer

I thank you LORD that I cannot lose, for I know that my inward being is being renewed day by day and your mercies are new for me every day. When I mess up and fail, the situation is always temporary because I knew that I will rise back up and win. I have put all my trust in you and cannot fail. Your glory will be seen through my life!

Faith

Mark 11:23-24
"For assuredly, I say to you, whoever says to this mountain, 'Be removed and be cast into the sea,' and does not doubt in his heart, but believes that those things he says will be done, he will have whatever he says. Therefore I say to you, whatever things you ask when you pray, believe that you receive them, and you will have them." - Mark 11:23-24 NKJV

Mark 9:23
"Jesus said to him, "If you can believe, all things are possible to him who believes."" - Mark 9:23 NKJV

Prayer

LORD I believe! Your word tells me that if I believe, then all things are possible, therefore today I make a decision to believe your word in my situation. Strengthen my faith that I may believe before I see the end of my faith, for in your kingdom, believing is seeing; I believe and therefore I receive it now in Jesus's name and I give you praise for it.

Family

Psalm 133:1
"Behold, how good and how pleasant *it is* for brethren to dwell together in unity!" – Psalm 133:1 NKJV

Mark 3:25
"And if a house is divided against itself, that house cannot stand." - Mark 3:25 NKJV

Ephesians 3:15-17

"from whom the whole family in heaven and earth is named, that He would grant you, according to the riches of His glory, to be strengthened with might through His Spirit in the inner man, that Christ may dwell in your hearts through faith; that you, being rooted and grounded in love," - Ephesians 3:15-17 NKJV

Prayer

Lord I know that you delight in unity and where there is unity, you readily pour out a blessing. I rebuke divisions among my family and I speak peace and unity only! You Oh LORD hand-picked my family for me and placed me in their midst for a purpose, thank you for my family wholeness; thank you that all things are working together for me and my whole family, from the least to the greatest.

Fear

Psalm 23:4

"Yea, though I walk through the valley of the shadow of death, I will fear no evil; For You are with me; Your rod and Your staff, they comfort me." - Psalms 23:4 NKJV

Romans 8:37-39

"Yet in all these things we are more than conquerors through Him who loved us. For I am persuaded that neither death nor life, nor angels nor principalities nor powers, nor things present nor things to come, nor height nor depth, nor any other created thing, shall be able to separate us from the love of God which is in Christ Jesus our Lord." - Romans 8:37-39 NKJV

Psalm 27:1-3

"The LORD is my light and my salvation; whom shall I fear? The LORD is the strength of my life; Of whom shall I be afraid? When the wicked came against me to eat up my flesh, my enemies and foes, they stumbled and fell. Though an army may encamp against me, my heart shall not fear; though war may rise against me, in this I will be confident."
- Psalms 27:1-3 NKJV

Prayer

I refuse to fear regardless of how things look right now, for though I walk through the valley of the shadow of death, I will fear no evil because you are with me. Nothing can separate me from your love oh LORD, not the visible and certainly not the invisible; whether I am awake or asleep, I am not afraid, for He who watches over me never sleeps nor slumbers. LORD, you are my hiding place, my secret weapon and my secret place of refuge in all seasons.

Finances

Proverbs 22:9

"He who has a generous eye will be blessed, for he gives of his bread to the poor." - Proverbs 22:9 NKJV

1 Timothy 5:8

"But if anyone does not provide for his own, and especially for those of his household, he has denied the faith and is worse than an unbeliever." - I Timothy 5:8 NKJV

1 Timothy 6:17-19

"Command those who are rich in this present age not to be haughty, nor to trust in uncertain riches but in the living

God, who gives us richly all things to enjoy. Let them do good, that they be rich in good works, ready to give, willing to share, storing up for themselves a good foundation for the time to come, that they may lay hold on eternal life." - I Timothy 6:17-19 NKJV

3 John 1:2
"Beloved, I pray that you may prosper in all things and be in health, just as your soul prospers." - III John 1:2 NKJV

Prayer

Thank you Lord that though I do not put my trust in money, you will bless me with lots of it, so that I may be a blessing to others. I thank You that I am Your faithful distribution centre in the earth and I have the power to help the poor and do good during my time here on earth. Teach me to be even more generous Oh Lord that I may lay up even more treasure in my heavenly storehouse by being a blessing here and now. I receive increase and overflow over everything I set my heart to do in Jesus' name.

Focus

Philippians 3:15-16
"Therefore let us, as many as are mature, have this mind; and if in anything you think otherwise, God will reveal even this to you. Nevertheless, to the degree that we have already attained, let us walk by the same rule, let us be of the same mind." - Philippians 3:15-16 NKJV

Prayer

Thank you LORD that I have a sound mind and there is no confusion within me. I am mature in my thinking and am not tossed about by different ideas but am focused on my goals and dreams. Thank you LORD that I have razor-sharp focus because my soul is anchored in you! Order my steps in your word dear Lord and I will not depart from your will and purpose for my life.

Forgiveness

Matthew 6:14-15
""For if you forgive men their trespasses, your heavenly Father will also forgive you. But if you do not forgive men their trespasses, neither will your Father forgive your trespasses." - Matthew 6:14-15 NKJV

Mark 11:25-26
""And whenever you stand praying, if you have anything against anyone, forgive him, that your Father in heaven may also forgive you your trespasses. But if you do not forgive, neither will your Father in heaven forgive your trespasses."" - Mark 11:25-26 NKJV

Prayer

LORD, help me to forgive those who have wronged me as it is not easy sometimes. I even have people in my life who keep locking themselves up in my jail of unforgiveness every time I release them! Help me to not get tired of letting them all go every time oh Lord. I know that if I do not forgive others, I will have no confidence to ask You for my own redemption and forgiveness.

Funerals

1 Thessalonians 4:13-18
"But I do not want you to be ignorant, brethren, concerning those who have fallen asleep, lest you sorrow as others who have no hope. For if we believe that Jesus died and rose again, even so God will bring with Him those who sleep in Jesus. For this we say to you by the word of the Lord, that we who are alive and remain until the coming of the Lord will by no means precede those who are asleep. For the Lord Himself will descend from heaven with a shout, with the voice of an archangel, and with the trumpet of God. And the dead in Christ will rise first. Then we who are alive and remain shall be caught up together with them in the clouds to meet the Lord in the air. And thus we shall always be with the Lord. Therefore comfort one another with these words." - I Thessalonians 4:13-18 NKJV

Prayer

This is a very difficult time for me and my family Lord as we have lost a loved one. Your word says that the death of a saint is a sweet thing to you but for me, it really hurts. I ask you to comfort me and my family during this time and be our rock and strength. I know that when you return in glory, those who have fallen asleep will rise first to meet You in the air and so I take comfort in knowing that you will make all things perfect in your time oh Lord, thank you. I receive healing and restoration now and I pray that Your supernatural joy be my strength in Jesus' name!

Friendship

Proverbs 27:9
"Ointment and perfume delight the heart, and the sweetness of a man's friend gives delight by hearty counsel." - Proverbs 27:9 NKJV

Psalm 133:1-3
"Behold, how good and how pleasant it is for brethren to dwell together in unity! It is like the precious oil upon the head, running down on the beard, the beard of Aaron, Running down on the edge of his garments. It is like the dew of Hermon, Descending upon the mountains of Zion; for there the LORD commanded the blessing— Life forevermore." - Psalms 133:1-3 NKJV

Prayer
Thank you Lord for giving me sweet friends who delight my heart; thank you for bringing the right people into my life and removing all the wrong ones. I pray that you will give me the wisdom and understanding to pick the right friends.

Giving

Luke 6:38
"Give, and it will be given to you: good measure, pressed down, shaken together, and running over will be put into your bosom. For with the same measure that you use, it will be measured back to you.'" - Luke 6:38 NKJV

2 Corinthians 9:6-9
"But this I say: He who sows sparingly will also reap sparingly, and he who sows bountifully will also reap

bountifully. So let each one give as he purposes in his heart, not grudgingly or of necessity; for God loves a cheerful giver. And God is able to make all grace abound toward you, that you, always having all sufficiency in all things, may have abundance for every good work. As it is written: "He has dispersed abroad, He has given to the poor; His righteousness endures forever."" - II Corinthians 9:6-9 NKJV

Acts 20:35
"I have shown you in every way, by labouring like this, that you must support the weak. And remember the words of the Lord Jesus, that He said, 'It is more blessed to give than to receive.' "" - Acts 20:35 NKJV

Prayer

I am a giver and a sower and I thank you for giving me the privilege to be a blessing. Because I am a giver, I believe I receive my harvest, in good measure, pressed down, shaken together and running over! I give joyfully because God loves a cheerful giver. As a support the weak and give to the poor, I believe that I am blessed and I thank you for your favourover my life in Jesus' name!

Giving up

2 Corinthians 4:16-18
"Therefore we do not lose heart. Even though our outward man is perishing, yet the inward man is being renewed day by day. For our light affliction, which is but for a moment, is working for us a far more exceeding and eternal weight of glory, while we do not look at the things which are seen, but at the things which are not seen. For the things which

are seen are temporary, but the things which are not seen are eternal." - II Corinthians 4:16-18 NKJV

Colossians 1:11-12
"Strengthened with all might, according to His glorious power, for all patience and longsuffering with joy; giving thanks to the Father who has qualified us to be partakers of the inheritance of the saints in the light." - Colossians 1:11-12 NKJV

Deuteronomy 31:6
"Be strong and of good courage, do not fear nor be afraid of them; for the LORD your God, He is the One who goes with you. He will not leave you nor forsake you.'" - Deuteronomy 31:6 NKJV

Isaiah 40:29-31
"He gives power to the weak, And to those who have no might He increases strength. Even the youths shall faint and be weary, and the young men shall utterly fall, but those who wait on the LORD Shall renew their strength; They shall mount up with wings like eagles, they shall run and not be weary, they shall walk and not faint." - Isaiah 40:29-31 NKJV

Prayer

I refuse to quit no matter how hard and complicated things are right now! My inward man is being renewed and my unseen victory is being transformed into my reality. Thank you LORD that you give me strength to keep going and not give up; thank you that You will never leave me nor forsake me. Give me the courage to keep walking and not grow weary; like an eagle, let me fly high as high can be.

Goals

Proverbs 15:22
"Without counsel, plans go awry, but in the multitude of counsellors they are established." - Proverbs 15:22 NKJV

Proverbs 16:3
"Commit your works to the LORD, and your thoughts will be established." - Proverbs 16:3 NKJV

Proverbs 13:16
"Every prudent man acts with knowledge, but a fool lays open his folly." - Proverbs 13:16 NKJV

Prayer

Thank you for the wisdom to plan with specific goals; thank you that you give me counsel that gets me established in life; And thank you that You give me knowledge to set smart goals that are specific, measurable, realistic and time-specific. Your word says it is for me to set goals and make plans but you Oh LORD bring them to pass in Jesus' name.

Gossip

Psalm 141:3-4
"Set a guard, O LORD, over my mouth; Keep watch over the door of my lips. Do not incline my heart to any evil thing, to practice wicked works with men who work iniquity; And do not let me eat of their delicacies." - Psalms 141:3-4 NKJV

Prayer

Lord, help me to watch my lips that I may not talk ugly about other people, clean my heart that I may only think good thoughts about others and keep me away from the company of gossipers and liars that I may keep myself clean and drama-free. I like my peace of mind.

Guidance

Isaiah 14:27
"For the LORD of hosts has purposed, and who will annul it? His hand is stretched out, and who will turn it back?"'"
Isaiah 14:27 NKJV

Isaiah 55:10-11
""For as the rain comes down, and the snow from heaven, and do not return there, but water the earth, and make it bring forth and bud, That it may give seed to the sower and bread to the eater, So shall My word be that goes forth from My mouth; It shall not return to Me void, But it shall accomplish what I please, And it shall prosper in the thing for which I sent it." - Isaiah 55:10-11 NKJV

Psalm 33:11-12
"The counsel of the LORD stands forever, the plans of His heart to all generations. Blessed is the nation whose God is the LORD, The people He has chosen as His own inheritance." - Psalms 33:11-12 NKJV

Prayer

No one can change what You have set in motion oh LORD and your word never returns back to you void but always gets the job done. Thank you for showing me through your word how to win in life and which way I should turn. Your counsel stands forever and I am blessed because you are my God; You have chosen me to be Your inheritance.

Grace

1 Corinthians 15:10
"But by the grace of God I am what I am, and His grace toward me was not in vain; but I laboured more abundantly than they all, yet not I, but the grace of God which was with me." - I Corinthians 15:10 NKJV

Ephesians 4:7
"But to each one of us grace was given according to the measure of Christ's gift." - Ephesians 4:7 NKJV

Prayer

I am all that I am only by Your grace O LORD and I am forever grateful for that! Give me more grace that I may win in life and that all may go well with me, for You give to everyone the measure of grace. Thank you for loving me and for giving me favour despite myself in Jesus' name.

Grief

1 Thessalonians 4:13
"But I do not want you to be ignorant, brethren, concerning those who have fallen asleep, lest you sorrow as others who have no hope." - I Thessalonians 4:13 NKJV

Psalm 9:9-10
"The LORD also will be a refuge for the oppressed, A refuge in times of trouble. And those who know Your name will put their trust in You; For You, LORD, have not forsaken those who seek You." - Psalms 9:9-10 NKJV

Prayer

My heart is so heavy and I feel so downcast Oh LORD, if ever I needed you, it is now. You are my refuge in troubled times and I put all my trust in You, for You will never forsake those who seek You. Thank you for Your comfort and love during this time of my life.

Guilt

2 Samuel 24:10
"And David's heart condemned him after he had numbered the people. So David said to the LORD, "I have sinned greatly in what I have done; but now, I pray, O LORD, take away the iniquity of Your servant, for I have done very foolishly."" - II Samuel 24:10 NKJV

Prayer

I confess my sins to you LORD and I surrender all my issues to You. I lay down all my guilt and pray that You take it all away in Jesus' name. Cleanse me by your blood that was shed on Calvary tree and I will be clean.

Happiness

2 Corinthians 7:13
"Therefore we have been comforted in your comfort. And we rejoiced exceedingly more for the joy of Titus, because his spirit has been refreshed by you all." - II Corinthians 7:13 NKJV

Psalm 16:11
"You will show me the path of life; In Your presence is fullness of joy; At Your right hand are pleasures forevermore." - Psalms 16:11 NKJV

Prayer

Comfort me oh LORD and fill my cup of joy today! I rejoice in you for You show me the path of life and I dwell in Your presence where there is fullness of joy; at your right hand, I enjoy pleasures forever more and so I am happy every day no matter what, thank you LORD.

Healing

Isaiah 53:5
"But He was wounded for our transgressions, He was bruised for our iniquities; The chastisement for our peace

was upon Him, and by His stripes we are healed." - Isaiah 53:5 NKJV

Psalm 146:8
"The LORD opens the eyes of the blind; The LORD raises those who are bowed down; The LORD loves the righteous." - Psalms 146:8 NKJV

Psalm 147:3
"He heals the brokenhearted and binds up their wounds." - Psalms 147:3 NKJV

Jeremiah 17:14
"Heal me, O LORD, and I shall be healed; Save me, and I shall be saved, forYou are my praise." - Jeremiah 17:14 NKJV

Prayer

Thank you LORD that regardless of what my diagnosis and prognosis are, by your stripes I am already healed! You bind up all my wounds and give total peace to my body; heal me O LORD and I shall be healed, save me and I will be saved, for you sent your word and healed my disease. I declare today that I will live and not die in Jesus' name!

Health

Exodus 23:25
""So you shall serve the LORD your God, and He will bless your bread and your water. And I will take sickness away from the midst of you." - Exodus 23:25 NKJV

3 John 1:2
"Beloved, I pray that you may prosper in all things and be in health, just as your soul prospers."
III John 1:2 NKJV

Prayer

Thank you LORD that I walk in perpetual divine health all the days of my life. I am prosperous in my soul and in my physical body for You bless my food and take sickness away from anything connected to me. I am totally untouchable when I am with You and You will never leave me nor forsake me, therefore, my health is guaranteed.

Heartbreak

Psalm 147:3
"He heals the brokenhearted and binds up their wounds."
Psalms 147:3 NKJV

Psalm 34:18-19
"The LORD is near to those who have a broken heart, and saves such as have a contrite spirit. Many are the afflictions of the righteous; But the LORD delivers him out of them all." - Psalms 34:18-19 NKJV

Psalm 73:26
"My flesh and my heart fail; But God is the strength of my heart and my portion forever." - Psalms 73:26 NKJV

Isaiah 41:10-11
"Fear not, for I am with you; Be not dismayed, for I am your God. I will strengthen you, Yes, I will help you, I will uphold you with My righteous right hand.' "Behold, all

those who were incensed against you shall be ashamed and disgraced; They shall be as nothing, and those who strive with you shall perish." - Isaiah 41:10-11 NKJV

Prayer

My God who heals the brokenhearted, I need You more than ever right now for I am in pain and my heart is hurting. I refuse to fear the worst during this time in my life for I know that Your right hand will uphold me and all my adversaries and haters will become as nothing; those who insist on continuing to hurt me shall have You to answer to and be removed. Please help my enemies to repent quickly before they are destroyed by your anointing!

Holy Spirit

John 16:14-15
"He will glorify Me, for He will take of what is Mine and declare it to you. All things that the Father has are Mine. Therefore I said that He will take of Mine and declare it to you." - John 16:14-15 NKJV

1 Corinthians 3:16
"Do you not know that you are the temple of God and that the Spirit of God dwells in you?" - I Corinthians 3:16 NKJV

Prayer

Holy Spirit, you are my best friend and my closest companion; help me to not grieve you that I may stay close to you and learn at your feet, for you know all things; you know the mind and heart of God and reveal all things to me every day. I love to fellowship with you and I thank you for choosing to dwell within me, I am your holy temple.

Homelessness

Psalm 34:9-10
"Oh, fear the LORD, you His saints! There is no want to those who fear Him. The young lions lack and suffer hunger; But those who seek the LORD shall not lack any good thing." - Psalms 34:9-10 NKJV

Psalm 23:1
"The LORD is my shepherd; I shall not want. He makes me to lie down in green pastures; He leads me beside the still waters." - Psalms 23:1-2 NKJV

Acts 17:26-28
"And He has made from one blood every nation of men to dwell on all the face of the earth, and has determined their pre-appointed times and the boundaries of their dwellings, so that they should seek the Lord, in the hope that they might grope for Him and find Him, though He is not far from each one of us; for in Him we live and move and have our being, as also some of your own poets have said, 'For we are also His offspring.'" - Acts 17:26-28 NKJV

Prayer

Because I seek you LORD, I will lack no good thing! You are my Shepherd and I shall not want, you make me lie down in green pastures and that means you have a home with my name on it and I receive it now by faith. My exact post code and address was even determined way before I was even born, before my parents looked at each other and said, "Hey..." You had already decided where my home will be and now I receive by faith that which You have already prepared for me. My home will not be repossessed; I will not be evicted and will never ever be homeless in Jesus' name! Instead, I will pay off other people's homes!

Hope

Hebrews 6:19
"This hope we have as an anchor of the soul, both sure and steadfast, and which enters the Presence behind the veil," - Hebrews 6:19 NKJV

Job 13:15
"Though He slay me, yet will I trust Him. Even so, I will defend my own ways before Him." - Job 13:15 NKJV

Prayer

My hope in You O LORD anchors my soul and therefore, I am not moved! I stand both sure and steadfast because you went behind the veil on my behalf and even though sometimes it feels like you are not listening or are taking too long, yet will I trust you with my whole life, I am confident and have no doubt that You will come through for me no matter what and I will not be put to shame!

Hurting

Psalm 23:4
"Yea, though I walk through the valley of the shadow of death, I will fear no evil; For You are with me; Your rod and Your staff, they comfort me." - Psalms 23:4 NKJV

Psalm 119:76-77
"Let, I pray, Your merciful kindness be for my comfort, According to Your word to Your servant. Let Your tender mercies come to me, that I may live; For Your law is my delight." - Psalms 119:76-77 NKJV

Psalm 9:9-10
"The LORD also will be a refuge for the oppressed, A refuge in times of trouble. And those who know Your name will put their trust in You; For You, LORD, have not forsaken those who seek You." - Psalms 9:9-10 NKJV

Prayer

Thank you LORD that You comfort me with Your tender mercies for your word is my delight. You are my refuge when life gets hard and I get hurt by situations and by other people, I trust in Your name and put my hope in You, for I know that you will never leave me nor forsake me!

Incarceration

Matthew 25:36-40
"I was naked and you clothed Me; I was sick and you visited Me; I was in prison and you came to Me.' "Then the righteous will answer Him, saying, 'Lord, when did we see You hungry and feed You, or thirsty and give You drink? When did we see You a stranger and take You in, or naked and clothe You? Or when did we see You sick, or in prison, and come to You?' And the King will answer and say to them, 'Assuredly, I say to you, inasmuch as you did it to one of the least of these My brethren, you did it to Me.'" - Matthew 25:36-40 NKJV

Psalm 107:8-16

"Oh, that men would give thanks to the LORD for His goodness, And for His wonderful works to the children of men! For He satisfies the longing soul, And fills the hungry soul with goodness. Those who sat in darkness and in the shadow of death, Bound in affliction and irons— Because they rebelled against the words of God, and despised the counsel of the Most High, Therefore He brought down their heart with labor; They fell down, and there was none to help. Then they cried out to the LORD in their trouble, And He saved them out of their distresses. He brought them out of darkness and the shadow of death, and broke their chains in pieces. Oh, that men would give thanks to the LORD for His goodness, and for His wonderful works to the children of men! For He has broken the gates of bronze, and cut the bars of iron in two." - Psalms 107:8-16 NKJV

Prayer

I messed up LORD and found myself in prison! I want to turn my life completely around, please help me. I know that You care about everyone including those of us who have gotten ourselves in trouble with the law because Your word says that You do. I cry to you LORD and thank you that though I have fallen down and have not had much help around me, You will save me from my distress and bring me out of darkness and the shadow of death, You will break my chains in pieces especially my inner chains; You will break my gates of bronze and cut the bars of iron in two! Thank you that I am free from within and when I get out, I will live to see the goodness of the LORD in the land of the living. I am a new creation in Christ; for my life is being restored and my mind is being renewed and I will never be the same ever again in Jesus' name!

Increase

1 Corinthians 3:7
"So then neither he who plants is anything, nor he who waters, but God who gives the increase." - I Corinthians 3:7 NKJV

Proverbs 13:11
"Wealth gained by dishonesty will be diminished, but he who gathers by labor will increase." - Proverbs 13:11 NKJV

Genesis 26:12-14
"Then Isaac sowed in that land, and reaped in the same year a hundredfold; and the LORD blessed him. The man began to prosper, and continued prospering until he became very prosperous; for he had possessions of flocks and possessions of herds and a great number of servants. So the Philistines envied him." - Genesis 26:12-14 NKJV

Prayer

I declare that wealth and riches are in my house and You have given increase to all my seed and my work O LORD. My labour shall not be in vain because Your blessing will guarantee my increase. Even in times of economic recession and austerity, I will still reap a 100 fold in Jesus' name!

Insecurity

Psalm 37:1-5
"Do not fret because of evildoers, nor be envious of the workers of iniquity. For they shall soon be cut down like the grass, and wither as the green herb. Trust in the LORD, and do good; Dwell in the land, and feed on His

faithfulness. Delight yourself also in the LORD, and He shall give you the desires of your heart. Commit your way to the LORD, Trust also in Him, and He shall bring it to pass." - Psalms 37:1-5 NKJV

Prayer

The world does not scare me and I am not envious of the wicked because the blessings that come from you O LORD adds no sorrow with it. I delight myself in You and You give me the desires of my heart; And as I commit my life and all my dealings into your hands, you cause me to succeed. Thank you LORD that I am secure in You!

Insomnia

Psalm 127:2
"It is vain for you to rise up early, to sit up late, to eat the bread of sorrows; For so He gives His beloved sleep." - Psalms 127:2 NKJV

Proverbs 3:24-27
"When you lie down, you will not be afraid; Yes, you will lie down and your sleep will be sweet. Do not be afraid of sudden terror, nor of trouble from the wicked when it comes; For the LORD will be your confidence, and will keep your foot from being caught. Do not withhold good from those to whom it is due, when it is in the power of your hand to do so." - Proverbs 3:24-27 NKJV

Psalm 4:8
"I will both lie down in peace, and sleep; For You alone, O LORD, make me dwell in safety."
Psalms 4:8 NKJV

Prayer

LORD, you give sleep to your beloved; therefore, I thank you that insomnia is not my portion! When I retire for bed, I will not be scared of any form of terror or nightmare. For God will not keep goodness from me as this is my due season; my God can and He will! I will have sweet sleep when I go to bed because I will always sleep in His peace.

Investments

Proverbs 21:20
"There is desirable treasure, and oil in the dwelling of the wise, but a foolish man squanders it." - Proverbs 21:20 NKJV

Proverbs 21:5
"The plans of the diligent lead surely to plenty, but those of everyone who is hasty, surely to poverty." - Proverbs 21:5 NKJV

Ecclesiastes 11:1-6
"Cast your bread upon the waters, for you will find it after many days. Give a serving to seven, and also to eight, for you do not know what evil will be on the earth. If the clouds are full of rain, they empty themselves upon the earth; And if a tree falls to the south or the north, in the place where the tree falls, there it shall lie. He who observes the wind will not sow, and he who regards the clouds will not reap. As you do not know what is the way of the wind, or how the bones grow in the womb of her who is with child, so you do not know the works of God who makes everything. In the morning sow your seed, and in the evening do not withhold your hand; For you do not know

which will prosper, either this or that, or whether both alike will be good." - Ecclesiastes 11:1-6 NKJV

Prayer

LORD, give me wisdom and courage to invest wisely and not squander everything you put in my hands; cause my plans to increase and be plentiful. As I invest in different places, may my investments grow and make me wealthy. Give me the wisdom and insight to know which way the wind is blowing regarding profits and exponential growth that I may know where to invest my money. Although men have no idea what investments will prosper and only take chances whether calculated or not, You O LORD know all things and You know exactly, which portfolio will profit me and bring me much increase in the earth.

Justice

Isaiah 61:8
""For I, the LORD, love justice; I hate robbery for burnt offering; I will direct their work in truth, and will make with them an everlasting covenant." - Isaiah 61:8 NKJV

Prayer

You O LORD love justice and I thank You that You will come through for me and I will get justice in my situation. Your covenant with me remains for all time and through every situation. I receive justice now by faith and thank you for my victory even before it is all done.

Kindness

Luke 6:35-36
"But love your enemies, do good, and lend, hoping for nothing in return; and your reward will be great, and you will be sons of the Most High. For He is kind to the unthankful and evil. Therefore be merciful, just as your Father also is merciful." - Luke 6:35-36 NKJV

Prayer

LORD, help me to show kindness to others, especially those who do not deserve it in the same way that You have been kind to me; help me to love my enemies, to bless those who curse me and to pray for those who mistreat me. I thank You that I have the courage and grace to show kindness and mercy to everyone around me.

Knowledge

Proverbs 1:5
"A wise man will hear and increase learning, and a man of understanding will attain wise counsel," - Proverbs 1:5 NKJV

Prayer

Thank you LORD that you give me knowledge to thrive in this life; thank you for being my greatest counsellor and for giving me understanding. I have knowledge beyond my education and experience and I receive answers now!

Loneliness

Psalm 68:5-6
"Sing to God, sing praises to His name; Extol Him who rides on the clouds, By His name YAH, And rejoice before Him. A father of the fatherless, a defender of widows, Is God in His holy habitation. God sets the solitary in families; He brings out those who are bound into prosperity; But the rebellious dwell in a dry land." - Psalms 68:4-6 NKJV

Isaiah 49:15-16
""Can a woman forget her nursing child, and not have compassion on the son of her womb? Surely they may forget, yet I will not forget you. See, I have inscribed you on the palms of My hands; Your walls are continually before Me." - Isaiah 49:15-16 NKJV

Psalm 27:10
"When my father and my mother forsake me, then the LORD will take care of me." - Psalms 27:10 NKJV

Prayer

I will never ever be lonely because You O LORD are always with me. You are the God that sets the lonely into families and I thank You that you will always bring the right people into my life at the right time. Like a woman does not forget her child in her womb, so will You not forget me O LORD, for You have inscribed me in the palm of Your hands. Even if my own flesh and blood forsake me, You will always take great care of me.

Love

Philippians 1:9
"And this I pray, that your love may abound still more and more in knowledge and all discernment," - Philippians 1:9 NKJV

John 3:16
"For God so loved the world that He gave His only begotten Son, that whoever believes in Him should not perish but have everlasting life." –John 3:16 NKJV

Prayer

I receive Your love into my life LORD that I may also be able to love others, for I can only give of what I have on the inside. You loved the world so much that You gave the ultimate gift of Your very own son, Jesus Christ, thank you for the greatest love offering ever given to mankind. I am indeed free because of Yourlove; for there is no fear in love and You O LORD are Love! I receive Your love today.

Lust

Job 31:1
""I have made a covenant with my eyes; Why then should I look upon a young woman?" - Job 31:1 NKJV

Prayer

Put a guard over my eyes LORD that I may not sin against you, for I have made a covenant with my eyes that I may not lust after those I am not married to. Thank You for giving me the courage to walk away and do the right thing.

Marriage

Genesis 2:24
"And they were both naked, the man and his wife, and were not ashamed." - Genesis 2:25 NKJ

Ecclesiastes 4:12
"Though one may be overpowered by another, two can withstand him. And a threefold cord is not quickly broken." - Ecclesiastes 4:12 NKJV

Mark 10:9
"Therefore what God has joined together, let not man separate.'" - Mark 10:9 NKJV

Prayer 1

As I enjoy being currently single, I thank You that someday I will marry and enjoy life with my perfect companion. Marriage is a gift from you O LORD and I thank you that You have prepared for me a wonderful life partner and I declare that I am on my way to a beautiful marriage. I believe I receive now in Jesus' name.

Prayer 2

I thank You for giving me a great companion in marriage and though we differ sometimes, I believe that we will enjoy a long loving life together by Your grace. Nothing shall separate us because You brought us together for You are in the middle of our marriage and a threefold cord is not easily broken. Our love is growing stronger and better and we have peace in our home and while one of us can chase a thousand, the two of us will chase 10 thousand and together, we win; our last word shall be victory!

Mental Health

Philippians 4:6-7
"Be anxious for nothing, but in everything by prayer and supplication, with thanksgiving, let your requests be made known to God; and the peace of God, which surpasses all understanding, will guard your hearts and minds through Christ Jesus." - Philippians 4:6-7 NKJV

Romans 8:6
"For to be carnally minded is death, but to be spiritually minded is life and peace." - Romans 8:6 NKJV

Isaiah 41:10
"Fear not, for I am with you; Be not dismayed, for I am your God. I will strengthen you, Yes, I will help you, I will uphold you with My righteous right hand.'" - Isaiah 41:10 NKJV

3 John 1:2
"Beloved, I pray that you may prosper in all things and be in health, just as your soul prospers." - III John 1:2 NKJV

2 Timothy 1:7
"Consider what I say, and may the Lord give you understanding in all things." - II Timothy 2:7 NKJV

Prayer

I have peace of mind that surpasses all understanding; peace that guards my heart and mind. You O LORD are my help and strength; my soul is prosperous and my mind is sound. Thank you that you give me understanding in all things; My mental health is excellent, I am not losing my mind and I am not confused in Jesus' name.

Mercy

2 Samuel 24:14
"Consider what I say, and may the Lord give you understanding in all things." - II Timothy 2:7 NKJV

Ephesians 2:4
"But God, who is rich in mercy, because of His great love with which He loved us," - Ephesians 2:4 NKJV

Titus 3:5
"not by works of righteousness which we have done, but according to His mercy He saved us, through the washing of regeneration and renewing of the Holy Spirit," - Titus 3:5 NKJV

Prayer

Thank you LORD for giving me mercy for every situation in my life and your mercies are new every morning; I thank you for loving me despite myself and for saving me through the blood of your son Jesus Christ and by Your Holy Spirit.

Ministry

Exodus 3:1
"Now Moses was tending the flock of Jethro his father-in-law, the priest of Midian.and he led the flock to the back of the desert, and came to Horeb, the mountain of God." - Exodus 3:1 NKJV

1 Corinthians 1:27-29
"But God has chosen the foolish things of the world to put to shame the wise, and God has chosen the weak things of the world to put to shame the things which are mighty; and the base things of the world and the things which are despised God has chosen, and the things which are not, to bring to nothing the things that are, that no flesh should glory in His presence." - I Corinthians 1:27-29 NKJV

Acts 9:15
"But the Lord said to him, "Go, for he is a chosen vessel of Mine to bear My name before Gentiles, kings, and the children of Israel." - Acts 9:15 NKJV

Prayer

As I step out into ministry and respond to Your call on my life, I believe that I have the anointing it takes to fulfil Your purpose for my life. You have chosen the foolish things of this world to use for Your glory and You picked me from the miry clay and set my feet on a higher ground. My life is an offering to You O LORD, use me to Your glory; O that I may make a mark on this generation that will never be erased; that I may live to change somebody's life and be a blessing to others in Jesus' name.

Miracles

Acts 3:16
"And His name, through faith in His name, has made this man strong, whom you see and know. Yes, the faith which comes through Him has given him this perfect soundness in the presence of you all." - Acts 3:16 NKJV

Jeremiah 32:27
""Behold, I am the LORD, the God of all flesh. Is there anything too hard for Me?" - Jeremiah 32:27 NKJV

Acts 19:11-12
"Now God worked unusual miracles by the hands of Paul, so that even handkerchiefs or aprons were brought from his body to the sick, and the diseases left them and the evil spirits went out of them." - Acts 19:11-12 NKJV

Prayer

There is power in the name of Jesus! I need a miracle right now and there is nothing too hard for You LORD, You have done unusual miracles before and I believe that You will do it again in my life. I receive breakthrough right now in Jesus' name; every valley shall be filled and every mountain shall be levelled and I win!

Miscarriage

Matthew 5:4
"Blessed are those who mourn, for they shall be comforted." - Matthew 5:4 NKJV

Romans 8:28

"And we know that all things work together for good to those who love God, to those who are the called according to His purpose." - Romans 8:28 NKJV

Isaiah 55:8-9

""For My thoughts are not your thoughts, nor are your ways My ways," says the LORD. "For as the heavens are higher than the earth, so are My ways higher than your ways, and My thoughts than your thoughts." - Isaiah 55:8-9 NKJV

Prayer

I have lost a child that I never had the privilege to meet and only You know why my child never made it into the world. I know that my baby is in glory with You and someday, we shall meet. All things work together for my good because I love You and are called according to Your purpose. Thank You for the strength to get through this season even as I look forward to better days that You have in store for me.

Missions

Matthew 28:19-20

"Go therefore and make disciples of all the nations, baptising them in the name of the Father and of the Son and of the Holy Spirit, teaching them to observe all things that I have commanded you; and lo, I am with you always, even to the end of the age." Amen." - Matthew 28:19-20 NKJV

Acts 1:8

"But you shall receive power when the Holy Spirit has come upon you; and you shall be witnesses to Me in

Jerusalem, and in all Judea and Samaria, and to the end of the earth.'"" - Acts 1:8 NKJV

Mark 16:15
"And He said to them, "Go into all the world and preach the gospel to every creature." - Mark 16:15 NKJV

Prayer

As I step out into missions by faith, thank You that the Holy Spirit will minister with me wherever I go and I have all my missionary needs already met, for with every vision, You give provision. Help me to preach your word without fear and with signs and wonders following in Jesus' name.

Mistakes

Psalm 37:24
"Though he fall, he shall not be utterly cast down; For the LORD upholds him with His hand." - Psalms 37:24 NKJV

Romans 8:1
"There is therefore now no condemnation to those who are in Christ Jesus, who do not walk according to the flesh, but according to the Spirit." - Romans 8:1 NKJV

Prayer

There is therefore no condemnation in my life because I am a child of God. All my mistakes are now in my past and forgetting the former things, I am moving forward! Though I make mistakes and fall, I will not be completely cast out, for You O LORD will uphold me with Your right hand and will not allow me to hit the ground nor drown in my errors. I believe I receive redemption now in Jesus' name!

Misunderstandings

Philippians 2:3
"Let nothing be done through selfish ambition or conceit, but in lowliness of mind let each esteem others better than himself." - Philippians 2:3 NKJV

John 15:13
"Greater love has no one than this, than to lay down one's life for his friends." - John 15:13 NKJV

Psalm 56:5
"All day they twist my words; All their thoughts are against me for evil." - Psalms 56:5 NKJV

Prayer

Help me to understand others quickly and gracefully and please give me favour to be understood wherever I go. My adversaries twist what I say and make up lies about me and all day long, they plan to do me wrong but I thank You that You've got my back and will exonerate me.

Nightmares

Proverbs 3:24
"Do not be afraid of sudden terror, Nor of trouble from the wicked when it comes;" - Proverbs 3:25 NKJV

Psalm 4:8
"I will both lie down in peace, and sleep; For You alone, O LORD, make me dwell in safety."
Psalms 4:8 NKJV

Psalm 91:5
"You shall not be afraid of the terror by night, Nor of the arrow that flies by day,"
Psalms 91:5 NKJV

Prayer

I am not afraid of any evil when I go to sleep because I know that You always watch over me whether I am awake or asleep. When my body is asleep, my spirit is always awake and I still win every fight even in my dreams! I am not afraid of having any nightmares because I am safe in your arms. Thank You for sweet dreams in Jesus' name.

New Things

2 Corinthians 5:17
"Therefore, if anyone is in Christ, he is a new creation; old things have passed away; behold, all things have become new." - II Corinthians 5:17 NKJV

Isaiah 43:19
"Behold, I will do a new thing, now it shall spring forth; Shall you not know it? I will even make a road in the wilderness and rivers in the desert." - Isaiah 43:19 NKJV

Prayer

Change is hard sometimes and can even be uncomfortable but I thank You that this is Your doing and I am not afraid, for You are doing a new thing in my life. I am excited about all the open doors that You are setting before me; the old is gone and I now embrace my new life and new opportunities in Jesus' name.

Natural disasters

Mark 13:7-9
"But when you hear of wars and rumours of wars, do not be troubled; for such things must happen, but the end is not yet. For nation will rise against nation, and kingdom against kingdom. And there will be earthquakes in various places, and there will be famines and troubles. These are the beginnings of sorrows. "But watch out for yourselves, for they will deliver you up to councils, and you will be beaten in the synagogues. You will be brought before rulers and kings for My sake, for a testimony to them." - Mark 13:7-9 NKJV

Matthew 24:7
"For nation will rise against nation, and kingdom against kingdom. And there will be famines, pestilences, and earthquakes in various places." - Matthew 24:7 NKJV

Prayer

The Bible says that in the last days, there will be natural disasters everywhere and Lord those days seem to be here now because lives are being lost every day due to natural disasters all over the world. I pray for every victim and their families, that You keep them safe and bring healing to the hurting and that You bring calm to every troubled nation.

Offense

Proverbs 19:11
"The discretion of a man makes him slow to anger, and his glory is to overlook a transgression." - Proverbs 19:11 NKJV

Ecclesiastes 7:21-22
"Also do not take to heart everything people say, lest you hear your servant cursing you. For many times, also, your own heart has known that even you have cursed others." - Ecclesiastes 7:21-22 NKJV

1 Peter 2:23
"who, when He was reviled, did not revile in return; when He suffered, He did not threaten, but committed Himself to Him who judges righteously;" - I Peter 2:23 NKJV

Prayer

LORD, help me to be slow to anger and keep calm whenever I have the invitation to lose my cool. Give me the patience and grace to overlook offence and not always take to heart what people say because I myself have wronged others in times past. Thank you for helping me to stay kind and quickly forgive others like You always forgive me.

Offerings

2 Corinthians 9:7
"So let each one give as he purposes in his heart, not grudgingly or of necessity; for God loves a cheerful giver." - II Corinthians 9:7 NKJV

Luke 6:38
"Give, and it will be given to you: good measure, pressed down, shaken together, and running over will be put into your bosom. For with the same measure that you use, it will be measured back to you.'" - Luke 6:38 NKJV

Proverbs 3:9-10
"Honor the LORD with your possessions and with the first fruits of all your increase; so your barns will be filled with plenty, and your vats will overflow with new wine." - Proverbs 3:9-10 NKJV

Prayer

Thank you that You give me seed to sow and I give with joy knowing that I will receive my harvest in good measure, pressed down, shaken together and running over! Thank You that as I give, my portfolio will always overflow with plenty, I declare that I am debt-free and that I have nothing missing and nothing broken in Jesus' name!

Orphans

James 1:27
"Pure and undefiled religion before God and the Father is this: to visit orphans and widows in their trouble, and to

keep oneself unspotted from the world." - James 1:27 NKJV

Psalm 68:5
"A father of the fatherless, a defender of widows, Is God in His holy habitation." - Psalms 68:5 NKJV

Psalm 10:14
"But You have seen, for You observe trouble and grief, to repay it by Your hand. The helpless commits himself to You; You are the helper of the fatherless." - Psalms 10:14 NKJV

Prayer

You are the Father to the fatherless and I know that I am never alone though I have lost my parents. Thank you for being my defense and for loving me more than anyone ever could. You are my help and the one who sustains me.

Overwhelmed

Isaiah 40:31
"But those who wait on the LORD Shall renew their strength; they shall mount up with wings like eagles, they shall run and not be weary, they shall walk and not faint." - Isaiah 40:31 NKJV

John 14:1
""Let not your heart be troubled; you believe in God, believe also in Me." - John 14:1 NKJV

Ephesians 6:10
"Finally, my brethren, be strong in the Lord and in the power of His might."- Ephesians 6:10 NKJV

Prayer

I feel like I am in way over my head LORD and my odds don't look too good, I don't even know whether I am coming or going sometimes but I thank You that You renew my strength because I wait on you, I shall rise higher like the eagle and never faint. I declare that I am strong in You and in the power of Your might; when I am weak, I am really strong because You are my pillar of strength!

Pain

Jeremiah 29:11
"For I know the thoughts that I think toward you, says the LORD, thoughts of peace and not of evil, to give you a future and a hope." - Jeremiah 29:11 NKJV

Psalm 34:18
"The LORD is near to those who have a broken heart, and saves such as have a contrite spirit." - Psalms 34:18 NKJV

Prayer

Even in my pain, You are still with me and I am comforted, for I know that Your plans for me are good and my future is sorted in You. The pain I feel is real but so are You my God and You are bigger than anything I can ever face in this life. Thank You for healing me from my pain and for making my joy complete and permanent in Jesus' name.

Parenting

Colossians 3:21
"Fathers, do not provoke your children, lest they become discouraged." - Colossians 3:21 NKJV

Exodus 20:12
""Honour your father and your mother, that your days may be long upon the land which the LORD your God is giving you." - Exodus 20:12 NKJV

Hebrews 12:11
"Now no chastening seems to be joyful for the present, but painful; nevertheless, afterward it yields the peaceable fruit of righteousness to those who have been trained by it." - Hebrews 12:11 NKJV

Prayer

Children are a beautiful blessing from You Lord and I thank You for mine. Help me to be a good parent; give me the patience and wisdom that I need to love my children the right way and raise them up in the way they should go. I thank You that my children will always honour me like I honour my own parents.

Patience

Ephesians 4:2
"with all lowliness and gentleness, with longsuffering, bearing with one another in love," - Ephesians 4:2 NKJV

Proverbs 15:18

"A wrathful man stirs up strife, but he who is slow to anger allays contention." - Proverbs 15:18 NKJV

Hebrews 6:12

"that you do not become sluggish, but imitate those who through faith and patience inherit the promises." - Hebrews 6:12 NKJV

Prayer
Thank You that I am patient and longsuffering, my temper is measured and I am slow to get angry. Help me not to walk in strife, help me to always remain calm and collected.

Peace

Philippians 4:7

"and the peace of God, which surpasses all understanding, will guard your hearts and minds through Christ Jesus." - Philippians 4:7 NKJV

Isaiah 26:3

"You will keep him in perfect peace, whose mind is stayed on You, because he trusts in You." - Isaiah 26:3 NKJV

Isaiah 54:10

"For the mountains shall depart and the hills be removed, But My kindness shall not depart from you, nor shall My covenant of peace be removed," Says the LORD, who has mercy on you." - Isaiah 54:10 NKJV

Prayer

Thank You LORD for giving me peace that surpasses all understanding and for keeping my heart and mind safe in Christ. You keep me in perfect peace because my mind is stayed on You and my trust and confidence are in your covenant, which remains for a lifetime and beyond. Thank You that regardless of what happens around me, you will never leave me nor forsake me all the days of my life.

Peer Pressure

Exodus 23:2
"You shall not follow a crowd to do evil; nor shall you testify in a dispute so as to turn aside after many to pervert justice." - Exodus 23:2 NKJV

Proverbs 1:10-15
"My son, if sinners entice you, do not consent. If they say, "Come with us, Let us lie in wait to shed blood; Let us lurk secretly for the innocent without cause; Let us swallow them alive like Sheol, And whole, like those who go down to the Pit; We shall find all kinds of precious possessions, We shall fill our houses with spoil; Cast in your lot among us, let us all have one purse"— My son, do not walk in the way with them, Keep your foot from their path;" - Proverbs 1:10-15 NKJV

Proverbs 13:20
"He who walks with wise men will be wise, but the companion of fools will be destroyed." - Proverbs 13:20 NKJV

Prayer

I receive wisdom and self-control to pick my friends correctly; to have the ability to make the right decisions even if it makes me unpopular with my friends. I know that sin looks very good and enticing but I have the courage to say no to bad behaviour and stay away from people that will corrupt my character. Thank You for insight, wisdom and understanding in Jesus' name.

Persecution

Revelation 2:10
"Do not fear any of those things which you are about to suffer. Indeed, the devil is about to throw some of you into prison, that you may be tested, and you will have tribulation ten days. Be faithful until death, and I will give you the crown of life." - Revelation 2:10 NKJV
John 15:18
""If the world hates you, you know that it hated Me before it hated you." - John 15:18 NKJV

2 Corinthians 12:10
"Therefore I take pleasure in infirmities, in reproaches, in needs, in persecutions, in distresses, for Christ's sake. For when I am weak, then I am strong." - II Corinthians 12:10 NKJV

Prayer

When I am persecuted, I will not be afraid because You keep me safe from evil. When I am hated for the gospel, I take comfort in knowing you were hated first. Thank You LORD that when I am weak, then I am really strong!

Perseverance

Romans 12:2
"And do not be conformed to this world, but be transformed by the renewing of your mind, that you may prove what is that good and acceptable and perfect will of God." - Romans 12:2 NKJV

Galatians 6:9
"And let us not grow weary while doing good, for in due season we shall reap if we do not lose heart." - Galatians 6:9 NKJV

James 1:12
"Blessed is the man who endures temptation; for when he has been approved, he will receive the crown of life which the Lord has promised to those who love Him." - James 1:12 NKJV

Prayer

Every day, I am being transformed into a new person and although I have gone through so much up to now, forgetting the past, I will continue to do good and press forward because my harvest is coming soon. This is my due season!

Pestilence

Luke 21:11
"And there will be great earthquakes in various places, and famines and pestilences; and there will be fearful sights and great signs from heaven." - Luke 21:11 NKJV

Psalm 91:6
"Nor of the pestilence that walks in darkness, Nor of the destruction that lays waste at noonday." - Psalms 91:6 NKJV

Revelation 3:10
"Because you have kept My command to persevere, I also will keep you from the hour of trial which shall come upon the whole world, to test those who dwell on the earth." - Revelation 3:10 NKJV

Prayer

I am free from the trouble of the ages and the pestilence that stalks our generation even as we live in these last days. And when the impending doom comes to the earth, I with all the saints will be safe in Your arms in glory, thank You LORD.

Phobias

2 Timothy 1:7
"For God has not given us a spirit of fear, but of power and of love and of a sound mind." - II Timothy 1:7 NKJV

1 John 4:18
"There is no fear in love; but perfect love casts out fear, because fear involves torment. But he who fears has not been made perfect in love." - I John 4:18 NKJV

Prayer

Fear is not my portion and today I gather up the courage to face all my fears with You on my side! Thank You LORD because there is no fear in love and Your love is perfect.

Pornography

Job 31:1
""I have made a covenant with my eyes; Why then should I look upon a young woman?" - Job 31:1 NKJV

Psalm 119:37
"Turn away my eyes from looking at worthless things, and revive me in Your way." - Psalms 119:37 NKJV

1 John 2:16
"For all that is in the world—the lust of the flesh, the lust of the eyes, and the pride of life—is not of the Father but is of the world." - I John 2:16 NKJV

1 Corinthians 6:18-20
"Flee sexual immorality. Every sin that a man does is outside the body, but he who commits sexual immorality sins against his own body. Or do you not know that your body is the temple of the Holy Spirit who is in you, whom you have from God, and you are not your own? For you were bought at a price; therefore glorify God in your body and in your spirit, which are God's." - I Corinthians 6:18-20 NKJV

Prayer

I have made a covenant with my eyes O LORD, that I may not sin against You by looking at images in lust. Please turn my eyes from admiring meaningless things and revive me from within, for all that is in the world: the lust of the flesh and of the eyes are not from You. Give me the strength to flee sexual immorality and look after my body, which is the temple of the Holy Spirit.

Poverty

Proverbs 22:22-23
"Do not rob the poor because he is poor, nor oppress the afflicted at the gate; For the LORD will plead their cause, and plunder the soul of those who plunder them." - Proverbs 22:22-23 NKJV

Proverbs 28:27
"He who gives to the poor will not lack, but he who hides his eyes will have many curses." - Proverbs 28:27 NKJV

Prayer

LORD, You are my provider and my provision. Thank You that I will not lack any good thing for You are Jehovah Jireh to me. Poverty is not my portion; wealth and riches shall instead be in my house. I declare that I am Your distribution center in the earth and I give generously to the poor and I fight for them. Your grace is sufficient for me.

Praise

Exodus 15:2
"The LORD is my strength and song, And He has become my salvation; He is my God, and I will praise Him; My father's God, and I will exalt Him." - Exodus 15:2 NKJV

Isaiah 63:7
"I will mention the loving-kindnesses of the LORD and the praises of the LORD, according to all that the LORD has bestowed on us, and the great goodness toward the house of Israel, Which He has bestowed on them according to His

mercies, According to the multitude of His loving-kindnesses." - Isaiah 63:7 NKJV

Psalm 150:6
"Let everything that has breath praise the LORD. Praise the LORD!" - Psalms 150:6 NKJV

Prayer

Praise is the offering I bring to You O LORD because You have been so good to me. I praise You with everything within me, for You chose me when I did not even deserve mercy and You picked me up at my lowest and set me up on a higher ground as Your own child.

Praying

2 Chronicles 7:14
"If My people who are called by My name will humble themselves, and pray and seek My face, and turn from their wicked ways, then I will hear from heaven, and will forgive their sin and heal their land." - II Chronicles 7:14 NKJV

1 John 5:14
"Now this is the confidence that we have in Him, that if we ask anything according to His will, He hears us." - I John 5:14 NKJV

Ephesians 6:18
"Praying always with all prayer and supplication in the Spirit, being watchful to this end with all perseverance and supplication for all the saints—" - Ephesians 6:18 NKJV

Prayer

Thank You that You always hear me when I pray and as I seek Your face, You will always answer my cry. LORD You have promised to hear from heaven, forgive my sins and heal me if I humble myself before you. And today, I am before Your face O LORD; I have every confidence that when I pray, You hear me. Thank You in Jesus' name.

Preaching

Mark 16:15
"And He said to them, "Go into all the world and preach the gospel to every creature." - Mark 16:15 NKJV

Matthew 28:18-20
"And Jesus came and spoke to them, saying, "All authority has been given to Me in heaven and on earth. Go therefore and make disciples of all the nations, baptising them in the name of the Father and of the Son and of the Holy Spirit, teaching them to observe all things that I have commanded you; and lo, I am with you always, even to the end of the age." Amen." - Matthew 28:18-20 NKJV

1 Timothy 4:13
"Till I come, give attention to reading, to exhortation, to doctrine." - I Timothy 4:13 NKJV

Prayer

I am called of You to preach the gospel and I have the fresh word that comes only from You and I thank You. I am a student of Your word and I diligently seek Your words of life. I receive authority to cast out demons and heal the sick even as I preach Your word.

Pregnancy

Jeremiah 1:5
""Before I formed you in the womb I knew you; Before you were born I sanctified you; I ordained you a prophet to the nations."" - Jeremiah 1:5 NKJV

Psalm 112:7
"He will not be afraid of evil tidings; His heart is steadfast, trusting in the LORD."
Psalms 112:7 NKJV

Isaiah 66:9
"Shall I bring to the time of birth, and not cause delivery?" says the LORD. "Shall I who cause delivery shut up the womb?" says your God." - Isaiah 66:9 NKJV

Prayer

Before I was even born, You knew me LORD and I thank You that You know my baby that I carry inside me. I am not afraid of any harm coming anywhere near my child, for when my due time comes, labour will go smoothly and there will be no complications because You will finish what You started and bring my baby into the world with joy and perfect health for both of us. Thank You LORD.

Progress

2 Corinthians 3:18
"But we all, with unveiled face, beholding as in a mirror the glory of the Lord, are being transformed into the same image from glory to glory, just as by the Spirit of the Lord."
- II Corinthians 3:18 NKJV

Psalm 92:12
"The righteous shall flourish like a palm tree; He shall grow like a cedar in Lebanon." - Psalms 92:12 NKJV

Proverbs 4:18
"But the path of the just is like the shining sun, that shines ever brighter unto the perfect day." - Proverbs 4:18 NKJV

Prayer

Every day I am being transformed to be more like Christ and share in his glory. I flourish like a palm tree and expand like the cedar tree from Lebanon, the most prodigious tree in the world! My future is like the bright shining sun that grows brighter every day. Thank You LORD that you not only know my future but You hold it in the palm of Your hands and because You live, I know that I can face tomorrow with the confidence of Your precious child.

Property

Psalm 24:1
"The earth is the LORD's, and all its fullness, the world and those who dwell therein." - Psalms 24:1 NKJV

Acts 17:26

"And He has made from one blood every nation of men to dwell on all the face of the earth, and has determined their pre-appointed times and the boundaries of their dwellings," - Acts 17:26 NKJV

Psalm 37:3

"Trust in the LORD, and do good; Dwell in the land, and feed on His faithfulness." - Psalms 37:3 NKJV

Prayer

I will never be without a roof over my head because the whole earth belongs you You my Father in heaven and You have already decided exactly where I will live and what piece of property I am to own in the earth. I trust in You and I believe that I will live to see the goodness of the LORD in the land of the living.

Prophecy

1 John 4:1

"Beloved, do not believe every spirit, but test the spirits, whether they are of God; because many false prophets have gone out into the world." - I John 4:1 NKJV

1 Corinthians 13:2

"And though I have the gift of prophecy, and understand all mysteries and all knowledge, and though I have all faith, so that I could remove mountains, but have not love, I am nothing." - I Corinthians 13:2 NKJV

Amos 3:7
"Surely the Lord GOD does nothing; Unless He reveals His secret to His servants the prophets." - Amos 3:7 NKJV

Prayer

Thank You for the gift of prophecy LORD and for revealing Your secrets to me. Help me to walk in love and be kind when I have a word for another person and help me discern all spirits that I may not stray away from Your word and Your perfect will for my life.

Promotion

Psalm 75:6
"For exaltation comes neither from the east nor from the west nor from the south." - Psalms 75:6 NKJV

Daniel 2:48
"Then the king promoted Daniel and gave him many great gifts; and he made him ruler over the whole province of Babylon, and chief administrator over all the wise men of Babylon." - Daniel 2:48 NKJV

Proverbs 18:16
"A man's gift makes room for him, and brings him before great men." - Proverbs 18:16 NKJV

Prayer

Promotion comes from You LORD and I receive elevation now in Jesus' name. Sharpen my gift that it may make more room for me. I know that regardless of how talented I am, unless You help me, I cannot and will not make it but I am on my way to the top because You are with me always.

Prosperity

Deuteronomy 28:8
""The LORD will command the blessing on you in your storehouses and in all to which you set your hand, and He will bless you in the land which the LORD your God is giving you." - Deuteronomy 28:8 NKJV

Proverbs 12:11
"He who tills his land will be satisfied with bread, but he who follows frivolity is devoid of understanding." - Proverbs 12:11 NKJV

Proverbs 10:22
"The blessing of the LORD makes one rich, and He adds no sorrow with it."
Proverbs 10:22 NKJV

2 Chronicles 20:20
"So they rose early in the morning and went out into the Wilderness of Tekoa; and as they went out, Jehoshaphat stood and said, "Hear me, O Judah and you inhabitants of Jerusalem: Believe in the LORD your God, and you shall be established; believe His prophets, and you shall prosper."" - II Chronicles 20:20 NKJV

Prayer

Thank you that you command a blessing on all that I do and on all the work of my hands. Your blessing makes me rich and adds no sorrow with it! I believe your word and therefore, I prosper; I am your distribution centre in the earth and I know that You will bring wealth my way because whatever You can get through me, You will get to me. I believe it and I receive now in Jesus' name.

Protection

2 Thessalonians 3:3
"But the Lord is faithful, who will establish you and guard you from the evil one." - II Thessalonians 3:3 NKJV

Deuteronomy 31:6
"Be strong and of good courage, do not fear nor be afraid of them; for the LORD your God, He is the One who goes with you. He will not leave you nor forsake you.'"
Deuteronomy 31:6 NKJV

Psalm 91:1-4
"He who dwells in the secret place of the Most High Shall abide under the shadow of the Almighty. I will say of the LORD, "He is my refuge and my fortress; My God, in Him I will trust." Surely He shall deliver you from the snare of the fowler and from the perilous pestilence. He shall cover you with His feathers, and under His wings you shall take refuge; His truth shall be your shield and buckler." - Psalms 91:1-4 NKJV

Prayer

LORD you protect me and guard me from evil; I am strong and courageous with no fear because You always go before me! You have promised to never leave me nor forsake me and because I have a personal relationship with you O LORD, I dwell in your secret place; You are my hiding place, my fortress. I have no doubt that You will always keep me safe and protect me from all harm whether spiritual or physical; seen or unseen.

Provision

2 Corinthians 9:8
"And God is able to make all grace abound toward you, that you, always having all sufficiency in all things, may have abundance for every good work." - II Corinthians 9:8 NKJV
Proverbs 10:22
"The blessing of the LORD makes one rich, And He adds no sorrow with it." - Proverbs 10:22 NKJV

Psalm 34:10
"The young lions lack and suffer hunger; But those who seek the LORD shall not lack any good thing." - Psalms 34:10 NKJV

Philippians 4:19
"And my God shall supply all your need according to His riches in glory by Christ Jesus." - Philippians 4:19 NKJV

Matthew 6:33
"But seek first the kingdom of God and His righteousness, and all these things shall be added to you." - Matthew 6:33 NKJV

Prayer

Thank you that you make all grace abound to me LORD, that I have all sufficiency and abound in all things. Your blessing has made me rich with no sorrow added,

Yousupply all my needs according to your riches in glory and as I seek your will and your kingdom first, all that I need shall be added to me in good measure, pressed down, shaken together and running over in Jesus' name.

Purpose

Exodus 9:16
"But indeed for this purpose I have raised you up, that I may show My power in you, and that My name may be declared in all the earth." - Exodus 9:16 NKJV

Job 42:2
""I know that You can do everything, and that no purpose of Yours can be withheld from You." - Job 42:2 NKJV

Proverbs 20:5
"Counsel in the heart of man is like deep water, but a man of understanding will draw it out." - Proverbs 20:5 NKJV

Isaiah 14:27
"For the LORD of hosts has purposed, and who will annul it? His hand is stretched out, and who will turn it back?"" - Isaiah 14:27 NKJV

Prayer

All that I am and all that I ever hope to be is tied up in your purpose for my life O LORD. Reveal your glory through me as I live out my purpose in the earth. Give me the wisdom and understanding that I need to live out my full potential and make my days count instead of just counting them. Nobody can change or nullify what you have purposed for my life. Thank you for choosing me and for giving me the courage to be all that you have designed for me to be. I will live my life deliberately and to your glory.

Quitting

Luke 9:62
"But Jesus said to him, "No one, having put his hand to the plow, and looking back, is fit for the kingdom of God."" - Luke 9:62 NKJV

Galatians 6:9
"And let us not grow weary while doing good, for in due season we shall reap if we do not lose heart." - Galatians 6:9 NKJV

2 Thessalonians 3:13
"But as for you, brethren, do not grow weary in doing good." - II Thessalonians 3:13 NKJV

1 Corinthians 9:24
"Do you not know that those who run in a race all run, but one receives the prize? Run in such a way that you may obtain it." - I Corinthians 9:24 NKJV

Prayer

This is so tough right now that I just want to throw in the towel LORD! But Your word says that I ought to persevere and not get tired of doing good, for I know that my harvest is imminent so I will keep standing and will not quit. Help me run my race to win and get the prize, for You who started a good work in me will surely finish what You started and I thank You that You are on my side!I will not hide, run away nor quit when the going gets tough but will put my trust in you and keep going. Victory is mine!

Racism

Acts 10:28
"Then he said to them, "You know how unlawful it is for a Jewish man to keep company with or go to one of another nation. But God has shown me that I should not call any man common or unclean." - Acts 10:28 NKJV

Acts 17:26
"And He has made from one blood every nation of men to dwell on all the face of the earth, and has determined their pre-appointed times and the boundaries of their dwellings," - Acts 17:26 NKJV

Prayer

Help me to be considerate and treat all people the same regardless of their colour or where they come from in the world; help me to be fair with everyone even when they sound or look different from me. For you created all men and even determined where we should all live in the earth that you created. You love everyone and so do I.

Regret

Philippians 3:13
"Brethren, I do not count myself to have apprehended; but one thing I do, forgetting those things which are behind and reaching forward to those things which are ahead," - Philippians 3:13 NKJV

2 Corinthians 7:10

"For godly sorrow produces repentance leading to salvation, not to be regretted; but the sorrow of the world produces death." - II Corinthians 7:10 NKJV

Isaiah 43:18-19

""Do not remember the former things, nor consider the things of old. Behold, I will do a new thing, now it shall spring forth; shall you not know it? I will even make a road in the wilderness and rivers in the desert." - Isaiah 43:18-19 NKJV

Prayer

Help me to forget the past and heal me from every painful memory. Instead of regret, I seek genuine repentance. May your blood wash me and make me clean, for whom the son sets free is free indeed, no longer to be subject to the yoke of slavery. Thank you LORD for your grace over my life.

Relationships

1 Peter 3:8-9

"Finally, all of you be of one mind, having compassion for one another; love as brothers, be tenderhearted, be courteous; not returning evil for evil or reviling for reviling, but on the contrary blessing, knowing that you were called to this, that you may inherit a blessing." - I Peter 3:8-9 NKJV

Proverbs 27:6

"Faithful are the wounds of a friend, But the kisses of an enemy are deceitful." - Proverbs 27:6 NKJV

Prayer

I speak wholeness to my relationships in Jesus' name. Instead of trouble and confusion, I have peace and love in all my circles and I thank You for giving me a lovely family and good faithful loving friends.

Repentance

Acts 3:19
"Repent therefore and be converted, that your sins may be blotted out, so that times of refreshing may come from the presence of the Lord," - Acts 3:19 NKJV

2 Corinthians 7:10
"For godly sorrow produces repentance leading to salvation, not to be regretted; but the sorrow of the world produces death." - II Corinthians 7:10 NKJV

Prayer

I confess my sins to you LORD and ask that you forgive me and wash me clean with the blood of Jesus that was shed for me and for my sins. I repent of my sins and I make a decision to leave my past behind and walk according to your word. Give me the strength and courage to keep my resolve and not go back to my past in Jesus' name.

Restlessness

Philippians 4:6
"Be anxious for nothing, but in everything by prayer and supplication, with thanksgiving, let your requests be made known to God;" - Philippians 4:6 NKJV

1 Timothy 6:6-8

"Now godliness with contentment is great gain. For we brought nothing into this world, and it is certain we can carry nothing out. And having food and clothing, with these we shall be content." - I Timothy 6:6-8 NKJV

2 Corinthians 12:9-10

"And He said to me, "My grace is sufficient for you, for My strength is made perfect in weakness." Therefore most gladly I will rather boast in my infirmities, that the power of Christ may rest upon me. Therefore I take pleasure in infirmities, in reproaches, in needs, in persecutions, in distresses, for Christ's sake. For when I am weak, then I am strong." - II Corinthians 12:9-10 NKJV

Romans 8:28

"And we know that all things work together for good to those who love God, to those who are the called according to His purpose." - Romans 8:28 NKJV

Psalm 46:10

"Be still, and know that I am God; I will be exalted among the nations, I will be exalted in the earth!" - Psalms 46:10 NKJV

Prayer

I am at peace and am not anxious for anything but bring all my concerns to you in prayer LORD. I make a decision to be content and to be happy with my lot. Even when I mess up, thank you that your grace is sufficient for me and in my weakness, your strength is made perfect. All things are working together for my good right now because I love you and I rest in your grace and mercy. Today, I will be still and know that Youalone are God; You are My God!

Restoration

Psalm 51:10-12
"Create in me a clean heart, O God, and renew a steadfast spirit within me. Do not cast me away from Your presence, and do not take Your Holy Spirit from me. Restore to me the joy of Your salvation, and uphold me by Your generous Spirit." - Psalms 51:10-12 NKJV

Psalm 80:7
"Restore us, O God of hosts; Cause Your face to shine, and we shall be saved!" - Psalms 80:7 NKJV

Prayer

Restoration is my blood-bought right and today I declare total recompense for everything that I have lost; I receive back a 100-fold in this life and then more when Christ returns in glory! Restore me O LORD, cause Your face to shine on me and I shall be restored in Jesus' name.

Riches

Psalm 112:3
"Wealth and riches will be in his house, and his righteousness endures forever." - Psalms 112:3 NKJV

Isaiah 45:3
"I will give you the treasures of darkness and hidden riches of secret places, that you may know that I, the LORD, Who

call you by your name, Am the God of Israel." - Isaiah 45:3
NKJV

Prayer

Take my issues and turn them into my greatest testimony
LORD. Create in me a new being who will bring glory to
your name. Forsake me not even though I have made many
mistakes. I am asking you for total restoration in every area
of my life right now. Let there be laughter in my house
again and may your joy be my strength! Thank you for
giving me treasures and riches; thank you that you know me
by name and I celebrate my future because it is in your
hands.

Sadness

Psalm 34:18
"The LORD is near to those who have a broken heart, and
saves such as have a contrite spirit." - Psalms 34:18 NKJV

Proverbs 17:22
"A merry heart does good, like medicine, But a broken
spirit dries the bones." - Proverbs 17:22 NKJV

Prayer

Take away a heavy heart from me and lift my mood with
your countenance LORD, for you are close to the brokenhearted and I am very vulnerable right now. I need you
more than ever, for you are my rock and my salvation, my
God in whom I trust. Thank you LORD.

Safety

Romans 8:31-32
"What then shall we say to these things? If God is for us, who can be against us? He who did not spare His own Son, but delivered Him up for us all, how shall He not with Him also freely give us all things?" - Romans 8:31-32 NKJV

Psalm 91:9-10
"Because you have made the LORD, who is my refuge, Even the Most High, your dwelling place, No evil shall befall you, Nor shall any plague come near your dwelling;" - Psalms 91:9-10 NKJV

Prayer

Heavenly Father, in you I find refuge and safety because I dwell in your secret place. You are my hiding place in times of trouble and evil cannot touch me. Who can rise up against me with you on my side, I am invincible and untouchable under your wings and I thank you LORD.

Salvation

Romans 10:10
"For with the heart one believes unto righteousness, and with the mouth confession is made unto salvation." - Romans 10:10 NKJV

John 3:3
"Jesus answered and said to him, "Most assuredly, I say to you, unless one is born again, he cannot see the kingdom of God."" - John 3:3 NKJV

Prayer

LORD I believe in Jesus Christ, I believe that he is your son whom you sent into the world to die for my sins and who rose back to life on the third day. Today, I ask him to come into my life and be my Lord and saviour; I am now born again and your child in Jesus' name. Thank you LORD!

Sex

Genesis 2:24-25
"Therefore a man shall leave his father and mother and be joined to his wife, and they shall become one flesh. And they were both naked, the man and his wife, and were not ashamed." - Genesis 2:24-25 NKJV

Prayer

Thank you for the gift of love-making and marriage; thank you that there is no fear or shame in your precious gift and I look forward to many years of a blissful married life.

Shame
Isaiah 54:4
""Do not fear, for you will not be ashamed; Neither be disgraced, for you will not be put to shame; For you will forget the shame of your youth, And will not remember the reproach of your widowhood anymore." - Isaiah 54:4 NKJV

Prayer

There is absolutely no shame in my future and no disgrace will follow my name, I will forget the shame of my youth and of all the mistakes that I have made so far in my life.

Thank you LORD that instead of shame, you have given me honour and instead of disgrace, you have given me glory; you have turned my mourning into dancing and traded my ashes for your everlasting beauty.

Sickness

Isaiah 53:5
"But He was wounded for our transgressions, He was bruised for our iniquities; The chastisement for our peace was upon Him, and by His stripes we are healed." - Isaiah 53:5 NKJV

Matthew 8:17
"that it might be fulfilled which was spoken by Isaiah the prophet, saying: "He Himself took our infirmities and bore our sicknesses."" - Matthew 8:17 NKJV

Exodus 15:26
"and said, "If you diligently heed the voice of the LORD your God and do what is right in His sight, give ear to His commandments and keep all His statutes, I will put none of the diseases on you which I have brought on the Egyptians. For I am the LORD who heals you."" - Exodus 15:26 NKJV

Prayer

I decree and declare that by your stripes I am healed! I refuse to believe the medical prognosis and choose to believe your word only. Your word says that you have already sent your word and healed my disease; that You Yourself took all my infirmities and bore all my sicknesses. I receive my healing by faith in Jesus' name!

Sin

Lamentations 1:20
""See, O LORD, that I am in distress; My soul is troubled; My heart is overturned within me, for I have been very rebellious. Outside the sword bereaves, at home it is like death." - Lamentations 1:20 NKJV

Acts 16:31
"So they said, "Believe on the Lord Jesus Christ, and you will be saved, you and your household."" - Acts 16:31 NKJV

Prayer

I am troubled within me because I have sinned against you LORD and my own conscious condemns me but I thank you that because of the death of Christ, I have redemption in you and your grace is sufficient for me. I confess my sins and ask you to please forgive me in Jesus' name.

Sorrow

Psalm 31:9
"Have mercy on me, O LORD, for I am in trouble; My eye wastes away with grief, Yes, my soul and my body!" - Psalms 31:9 NKJV

Prayer

I am struck with sorry as my issues overwhelm me, my eyes barely have any more tears left to cry and I have trouble breathing because of the lump in my throat that now feels like a growth! Take away the sadness and the pain that I may laugh again O LORD, for your joy is my strength.

Strength

Philippians 4:13
"I can do all things through Christ who strengthens me." - Philippians 4:13 NKJV

Isaiah 40:29-31
"He gives power to the weak, And to those who have no might He increases strength. Even the youths shall faint and be weary, and the young men shall utterly fall, but those who wait on the LORD Shall renew their strength; They shall mount up with wings like eagles, They shall run and not be weary, They shall walk and not faint." - Isaiah 40:29-31 NKJV

Isaiah 41:10
"Fear not, for I am with you; Be not dismayed, for I am your God. I will strengthen you, Yes, I will help you, I will uphold you with My righteous right hand.'" - Isaiah 41:10 NKJV

Prayer

I declare that I can do all things through Christ who gives me strength. Thank you LORD for giving me power; when I am weak; for renewing my strength when I am on the brink of collapsing; for causing me to soar like the eagle and for upholding me with your righteous hand. I receive supernatural strength now in Jesus' name.

Stress

Philippians 4:6-7
"Be anxious for nothing, but in everything by prayer and supplication, with thanksgiving, let your requests be made known to God; and the peace of God, which surpasses all understanding, will guard your hearts and minds through Christ Jesus." - Philippians 4:6-7 NKJV

John 14:1
""Let not your heart be troubled; you believe in God, believe also in Me."
John 14:1 NKJV

1 Peter 5:7
"casting all your care upon Him, for He cares for you." - I Peter 5:7 NKJV

Prayer

I declare that I am too blessed to be stressed and anxiety is not my portion! I refuse to worry because my hope is in you LORD. Thank you for giving me peace that surpasses all understanding, my heart is not troubled because I believe in you and you care for me. I live in a stress-free zone!

Success

Psalm 118:25
"Save now, I pray, O LORD; O LORD, I pray, send now prosperity." - Psalms 118:25 NKJV

Joshua 1:8

"This Book of the Law shall not depart from your mouth, but you shall meditate in it day and night, that you may observe to do according to all that is written in it. For then you will make your way prosperous, and then you will have good success." - Joshua 1:8 NKJV

Genesis 39:2-4

"The LORD was with Joseph, and he was a successful man; and he was in the house of his master the Egyptian. And his master saw that the LORD was with him and that the LORD made all he did to prosper in his hand. So Joseph found favour in his sight, and served him. Then he made him overseer of his house, and all that he had he put under his authority." - Genesis 39:2-4 NKJV

Prayer

Send now prosperity O LORD even as I stand on your word. I believe there is only good success in my future. Thank you for your blessing that causes me to prosper, like you were with your servant Joseph, so are you with me in all that I do. I surrender all my work into your hands and ask that you increase me more and more in Jesus' name.

Suicide

Psalm 34:17-19

"The righteous cry out, and the LORD hears, and delivers them out of all their troubles. The LORD is near to those who have a broken heart, and saves such as have a contrite spirit. Many are the afflictions of the righteous; But the LORD delivers him out of them all." - Psalms 34:17-19 NKJV

Exodus 14:14

"The LORD will fight for you, and you shall hold your peace."" - Exodus 14:14 NKJV

Prayer

My heart is troubled and I am struck with deep sorrow that I just do not see any reason for living anymore, please help me LORD and give me the courage to stay alive; the courage to reject harmful suggestions of self-harm. You are always near the broken-hearted and will save me in my weakest hour. I receive peace of mind now in Jesus' name.

Tears

Psalm 56:8-10

"You number my wanderings; Put my tears into Your bottle; Are they not in Your book? When I cry out to You, Then my enemies will turn back; This I know, because God is for me. In God (I will praise His word), In the LORD (I will praise His word)," - Psalms 56:8-10 NKJV

Psalm 126:6

"He who continually goes forth weeping, Bearing seed for sowing, Shall doubtless come again with rejoicing, bringing his sheaves with him." - Psalms 126:6 NKJV

Psalm 30:2-5

"O LORD my God, I cried out to You, And You healed me. O LORD, You brought my soul up from the grave; You have kept me alive, that I should not go down to the pit. Sing praise to the LORD, you saints of His, and give thanks at the remembrance of His holy name. For His anger is but for a moment, His favour is for life; Weeping may endure for a night, but joy comes in the morning." - Psalms 30:2-5 NKJV

Prayer

God you hear me when I cry and you will answer me when I call for my tears will not last forever, joy shall surely fill my heart. Heal me O LORD as I cry out to you; wipe away every tear from my eyes. Your anger lasts only for a short while but your joy comes in the morning; you will turn my mourning into dancing and I believe it, therefore, I receive.

Temptation

Romans 8:37
"Yet in all these things we are more than conquerors through Him who loved us." - Romans 8:37 NKJV

Hebrews 2:18
"For in that He Himself has suffered, being tempted, He is able to aid those who are tempted." - Hebrews 2:18 NKJV

Hebrews 4:15-16
"For we do not have a High Priest who cannot sympathise with our weaknesses, but was in all points tempted as we are, yet without sin. Let us therefore come boldly to the throne of grace, that we may obtain mercy and find grace to help in time of need." - Hebrews 4:15-16 NKJV

Prayer

I do get tempted sometimes but I thank you that I have the strength and courage to say no to sin and overcome temptation. I am more than a conqueror because I have a high priest in Christ who understands my every day challenges, having gone through various temptation and overcoming every single one of them; a high priest that can be touched by my feelings. Thank you LORD.

Thanksgiving

Psalm 69:30
"I will praise the name of God with a song, and will magnify Him with thanksgiving." - Psalms 69:30 NKJV

Psalm 100:4-5
"Enter into His gates with thanksgiving, and into His courts with praise. Be thankful to Him, and bless His name. For the LORD is good; His mercy is everlasting, and His truth endures to all generations." - Psalms 100:4-5 NKJV

Prayer

I may not have everything I want and need but I thank you for all that I have O LORD; today, my heart is filled with gratitude because you have been good to me despite my shortcomings. I will enter your gates with thanksgiving in my heart and enter your gates with praise, for you are good and your mercy endures forever!

The Future

Jeremiah 29:11-12
"For I know the thoughts that I think toward you, says the LORD, thoughts of peace and not of evil, to give you a future and a hope. Then you will call upon Me and go and pray to Me, and I will listen to you." - Jeremiah 29:11-12 NKJV

Prayer

Because you are my God and are alive forever more, I know that I can confidently face the future and therefore, I am not afraid of it. Your word says that you hold my future in your hands and your plans for me are good and are to give me an expected end. Thank you that you hear me when I pray, I give you praise now in Jesus' name.

Thoughts

Proverbs 12:5
"The thoughts of the righteous are right, but the counsels of the wicked are deceitful." - Proverbs 12:5 NKJV

Proverbs 15:28
"The heart of the righteous studies how to answer, but the mouth of the wicked pours forth evil." - Proverbs 15:28 NKJV

Prayer

I thank you that you order my steps in your ways LORD and my mind is fixed on you; therefore, you keep me in perfect peace. Please put a guard over my mind that I may not lose my way and think bad things. I declare that my thoughts are righteous because I am the righteousness of God in Christ; I am the temple of the Holy Spirit.

Tithes

Genesis 28:22
"And this stone which I have set as a pillar shall be God's house, and of all that You give me I will surely give a tenth to You."" - Genesis 28:22 NKJV

Malachi 3:10
"Bring all the tithes into the storehouse, that there may be food in My house, and try Me now in this," Says the LORD of hosts, "If I will not open for you the windows of heaven And pour out for you such blessing That there will not be room enough to receive it." - Malachi 3:10 NKJV

Prayer

Father, I know that I do not live by the law in the new covenant but I still choose to bring my tithes into your store house that there may be plenty in your house. Thank you that as I do so, you will open the floodgates of blessing in my life that will overflow to the point that I will not have room to contain it all. I believe I receive my harvest now.

Travelling

Psalm 89:15-17
"Blessed are the people who know the joyful sound! They walk, O LORD, in the light of Your countenance. In Your name they rejoice all day long, and in Your righteousness they are exalted. For You are the glory of their strength, and in Your favour our horn is exalted." - Psalms 89:15-17 NKJV

Zechariah 10:12

""So I will strengthen them in the LORD, and they shall walk up and down in His name," Says the LORD." - Zechariah 10:12 NKJV

Prayer

LORD I surrender my journey into your hands and I travel, I thank you that I have your favour and your face shines upon me, for you are the glory of my strength. No harm will come to me and those around me, I am safe in your arms because you are a good God and you care for me.

Unbelief

Hebrews 3:12-13

"Beware, brethren, lest there be in any of you an evil heart of unbelief in departing from the living God; but exhort one another daily, while it is called "Today," lest any of you be hardened through the deceitfulness of sin." - Hebrews 3:12-13 NKJV

Prayer

I believe you above everything that surrounds me LORD; I trust your word only and ask that you help my unbelief. Sometimes, things get so hard that I find it hard to believe that you still care and that you will come through for me. Even when I pray, there are times when it feels like there is only a ceiling above me but I know that your word says that you will never leave me nor forsake me and I choose to believe your word despite how I feel for I do not walk by how I feel nor what I see, I walk by faith.

Violence

Psalm 55:8-9
"I would hasten my escape from the windy storm and tempest." Destroy, O Lord, and divide their tongues, for I have seen violence and strife in the city." - Psalms 55:8-9 NKJV

Prayer

No violence shall come near my dwelling in Jesus' name! I am redeemed from destruction and I will live to fulfil the purpose of God for my life in peace and safety. Thank you LORD for putting a hedge of protection around me!

Vision

Habakkuk 2:3
"For the vision is yet for an appointed time; But at the end it will speak, and it will not lie. Though it tarries, wait for it; Because it will surely come, it will not tarry." - Habakkuk 2:3 NKJV

Prayer

I thank you LORD that I will live a full life; a life of purpose, inspired by vision. Sometimes, it seems like my dreams are taking too long to happen but I believe your word and my destiny will be accomplished. I will live to make a mark in the earth that will never be erased; I have zeal with knowledge and understanding and have the wisdom to set strategic goals to ensure my success.

Weakness

1 Corinthians 1:27
"But God has chosen the foolish things of the world to put to shame the wise, and God has chosen the weak things of the world to put to shame the things which are mighty;" - I Corinthians 1:27 NKJV

2 Corinthians 12:10
"Therefore I take pleasure in infirmities, in reproaches, in needs, in persecutions, in distresses, for Christ's sake. For when I am weak, then I am strong." - II Corinthians 12:10 NKJV

Prayer

When I am weak then I am really strong for you O LORD are the strength of my life. You are the God who takes the foolishness of this world in order to confound the wisdom of this world and I thank you for choosing me despite myself. My victory brings glory to your precious name.

Wealth

Psalm 112:3
"Wealth and riches will be in his house, and his righteousness endures forever." - Psalms 112:3 NKJV

Philippians 4:6-7
"Be anxious for nothing, but in everything by prayer and supplication, with thanksgiving, let your requests be made known to God; and the peace of God, which surpasses all understanding, will guard your hearts and minds through Christ Jesus." - Philippians 4:6-7 NKJV

Proverbs 10:22
"The blessing of the LORD makes one rich, And He adds no sorrow with it." - Proverbs 10:22 NKJV

Prayer

Wealth and riches are in my house and I will never lack any good thing because your blessing makes me rich and adds no sorrow with it. Whatever I touch will prosper and you will bless the work of my hands because you love me. There is no God like you and I praise you in advance for prospering me beyond my wildest dreams in Jesus' name.

Widows

Psalm 68:5
"A father of the fatherless, a defender of widows, Is God in His holy habitation." - Psalms 68:5 NKJV

Deuteronomy 10:18
"He administers justice for the fatherless and the widow, and loves the stranger, giving him food and clothing." - Deuteronomy 10:18 NKJV

Psalm 146:9
"The LORD watches over the strangers; He relieves the fatherless and widow; But the way of the wicked He turns upside down." - Psalms 146:9 NKJV

Proverbs 15:25
"The LORD will destroy the house of the proud; But He will establish the boundary of the widow." - Proverbs 15:25 NKJV

Prayer

LORD you are the defender and provider of justice to the widows and you watch over my life; you are my relief and the God who establishes me in the earth. There is none like you and I give you praise for all you have done for me. Your rod and your stuff, they comfort me and you make all things beautiful for me in your time.

Wisdom

Proverbs 11:14
"Where there is no counsel, the people fall; But in the multitude of counselors there is safety." - Proverbs 11:14 NKJV

Proverbs 15:22
"Without counsel, plans go awry, but in the multitude of counselors they are established." - Proverbs 15:22 NKJV

Proverbs 4:7
"Wisdom *is* the principal thing;*therefore* get wisdom.And in all your getting, get understanding." – Proverbs 4:7 NKJV

Prayer

Wisdom is the principle thing therefore LORD I choose to get wisdom and in all my getting, I get understanding! Thank you for being my greatest counsellor, with you on my side, I will never lose my way but will flourish and soar high like an eagle. I am wise beyond my years and my understanding is beyond my experience because you are on my side. I receive wisdom for every area of my life in Jesus' name.

Work

Psalm 128:2
"When you eat the labor of your hands, you shall be happy, and it shall be well with you." - Psalms 128:2 NKJV

Proverbs 14:23
"In all labor there is profit, but idle chatter leads only to poverty." - Proverbs 14:23 NKJV

Ephesians 4:28
"Let him who stole steal no longer, but rather let him labor, working with his hands what is good, that he may have something to give him who has need." - Ephesians 4:28 NKJV

Prayer

Help me find joy in my labour LORD, sometimes I do not really like my job but I thank you that my career will prosper because I do all my work as unto you. I will flourish in my work and will be a blessing to other people around me. Thank you that you bless the work of my hands.

Yielding to God

Ephesians 5:27
"that He might present her to Himself a glorious church, not having spot or wrinkle or any such thing, but that she should be holy and without blemish." - Ephesians 5:27 NKJV

Prayer

I yield to you LORD and surrender my life entirely into your hands, all that I am and all that I ever hope to be, I give you. My dreams and ambitions are at your feet, that I may be holy and without blemish; glorious in the earth even as my life brings honour to your name.

Yokes

Isaiah 10:27
"It shall come to pass in that day that his burden will be taken away from your shoulder, and his yoke from your neck,and the yoke will be destroyed because of the anointing oil." - Isaiah 10:27 NKJV

2 Corinthians 10:4-5
For the weapons of our warfare *are* not carnal but mighty in God for pulling down strongholds, casting down arguments and every high thing that exalts itself against the knowledge of God, bringing every thought into captivity to the obedience of Christ. – 2 Corinthians 10:4-5 NKJV

Prayer

Thank you LORD, that your anointing removes every burden from my life and destroys every yoke! I decree and declare that every stronghold in my life and my family is coming down in Jesus' name. No weapon formed against me shall prosper, it just will not work, for you will do what you said you will do LORD; You will come through for me. I receive breakthrough now and I declare that I win, for the weapons of my warfare are mighty and strong to the pulling down of all strongholds!

Zeal

Romans 12:11
"not lagging in diligence, fervent in spirit, serving the Lord;" - Romans 12:11 NKJV

Romans 10:2-3
For I bear them witness that they have a zeal for God, but not according to knowledge. For they being ignorant of God's righteousness, and seeking to establish their own righteousness, have not submitted to the righteousness of God. – Romans 10:2-3 NKJV

Prayer

Oh that my zeal will not be without knowledge but that I may flourish in knowing exactly who I am even as I go after my dreams. Give me the focus that I need to go after life with everything I've got. I am diligent and fervent in spirit even as I serve you; Your zeal O LORD consumes me and gives me amazing zest for life as my youth is renewed every day like the eagle's.

Epilogue

I hope you have enjoyed reading Kingdom Prayers and your prayer life is much richer because of it. Keep standing on the word and never pray outside the confines of the word of God ever again! My prayer for you as you hold this precious book whether to pass it on and bless somebody else or to revisit its contents whenever you need direction, is that you will live a life that is full and stress-free knowing that you have a Father in heaven who cares about you dearly and wants things to be well with you. Jesus came that you may have life in abundance and after all is said and done; your last word shall indeed be victory! Declare with me please, "Thank you LORD, for choosing me despite myself. Thank you that your promises to me are always yes and amen because I trust on your word. I live my life without fear or shame because I know that you are always with me. Help me to develop an even deeper walk with you that I may live to see your goodness in the land of the living. I rejoice and praise you before a thing is done and before I see any evidence because I believe that you are faithful and will come through for me, I do not walk by sight nor by what I feel, I walk by faith! You are my portion and the length of my days and I rest in your presence in Jesus' name, Amen." Remain blessed and keep the faith always. Remember, God only listens to prayers said in His name and based on His word, everything else is just talk.

Look out for my next book - How to UNLEASH your destiny: Live a life of purpose! Coming soon to a bookstore near you and on all reputable online platforms.

Printed in Great Britain
by Amazon